My testimonial to a trustworthy man … Alan LeVar.

I was raised in a time when a man's word was his bond. That's all I have ever known from the time I could remember until now, here I am at age 66. During those years I have witnessed men in all professions choose to sell their integrity over doing what is right. I can say without any hesitation that Alan Levar still stands for what is right. What better words can be said about a man?

—Larry Cole, president, *Trucking Experts Inc.*

No one in their right mind plans for a collision of any kind, let alone one with one of those gargantuan semi-tractor-trailers thundering down the interstate in every region of the country. Yet collisions do happen. When they do, what you do immediately is of critical importance. Attorney Alan LeVar's No Accidents—Only Collisions delivers essential advice and a comprehensive guide to protecting you and the people you love and getting them access to the medical attention and other services when they are needed most.

—R.B. Scott, journalist and author of

Mitt Romney: An Inside Look at the Man and His Politics

As a former insurance claims adjuster and currently practicing attorney, I understand the confusion, stress, and fear that come with being involved in a collision. I recommend having someone with the right experience and proven results on your side. Whether you have been involved in a tractor-trailer collision yourself or are in the business of advising other individuals who have, I am confident you will find this book to be a valuable resource as you determine the appropriate course of action for your unique situation.

—Douglas McCash

THERE ARE
NO ACCIDENTS
ONLY
COLLISIONS

THERE ARE NO ACCIDENTS ONLY COLLISIONS

WHAT YOU NEED TO KNOW IF YOU ARE HIT BY A TRACTOR-TRAILER

ALAN LEVAR

Published by Advantage, Charleston, South Carolina.
Member of Advantage Media Group.

ADVANTAGE is a registered trademark and the Advantage colophon is a trademark of Advantage Media Group, Inc.

Printed in the United States of America.

ISBN: 978-1-59932-556-9
LCCN: 2015944792

This publication is designed to provide accurate and authoritative information in regard to the subject matter covered. It is sold with the understanding that the publisher is not engaged in rendering legal, accounting, or other professional services. If legal advice or other expert assistance is required, the services of a competent professional person should be sought.

Advantage Media Group is proud to be a part of the Tree Neutral® program. Tree Neutral offsets the number of trees consumed in the production and printing of this book by taking proactive steps such as planting trees in direct proportion to the number of trees used to print books. To learn more about Tree Neutral, please visit www.treeneutral.com. To learn more about Advantage's commitment to being a responsible steward of the environment, please visit www.advantagefamily.com/green

Advantage Media Group is a publisher of business, self-improvement, and professional development books and online learning. We help entrepreneurs, business leaders, and professionals share their Stories, Passion, and Knowledge to help others Learn & Grow. Do you have a manuscript or book idea that you would like us to consider for publishing? Please visit advantagefamily.com or call 1.866.775.1696.

TABLE OF CONTENTS

INTRODUCTION

The people who have had and continue to have the greatest influence on my life have great empathy for the average guy, the underdogs of the world. Their examples continue to influence me and have led me to where I am now: representing people hurt in horrific collisions. That is part of why I wrote this book: a primer for all those who are dealing with pushy claims adjusters, attorneys, law enforcement, and medical providers and trying to put their life back together. I have seen the devastation in my own family, both before I went to law school and while I was in law school.

When you are hit by a tractor-trailer or big rig or whatever you prefer to call these large trucks, the relative size of the truck that hits you is a metaphor for the issues you will soon face. The company behind that truck not only had a truck on the road ten times the size of your vehicle but has 100 times the resources to investigate, deny, delay, or defend any claim and to prevent a level playing field. I know. I have seen it, and my family has experienced it.

My father had polio as a young boy. Somewhere along the way, he developed great empathy for the average American, the underdog. He understood the need for provisions in our law that protected even the weakest among us. He taught constitutional law for 25 years and taught me from an early age the value of this country, our Constitution, and the provisions in it that protected the average person. He had a great respect for the Bill of Rights, including the seventh-amendment right to a jury trial, and saw that amendment as invaluable in protecting our other rights and liberties.

So we talked often about law and about helping people. He instilled that in me, and because of that, I always knew I wanted to be a lawyer. I remember when I was in high school I saw the movie *Ghandi*. Mahatma Gandhi, of course, was an attorney. This became very relevant to me because his first protest was in South Africa, where I landed as a 19-year-old missionary in 1989. I actually got there a month before Nelson Mandela was released from prison on Robben Island. I got to witness a remarkable time in that country's history and see how South Africa made a peaceful transition to democracy as India had done.

I think that successful transition was due, in large part, to the checks and balances in place in their system of government, the legal system that had been in place, and the work that had been done by so many attorneys in laying the groundwork for that transition.

One of my greatest regrets was not wrangling myself into the Johannesburg soccer stadium to hear Nelson Mandela speak a week after he was released. I wish, in retrospect, that I had been more persistent. I regret not having participated in that historic event, but I did get to talk to many people as the transition was happening, and those are memories that I cherish, and they intensified my desire to practice law and serve the underrepresented.

When I got back to Arkansas, I thought I might like to practice international law; I wanted to fight those sorts of issues and help people deal with those sorts of problems. So I majored in international relations, went through law school, got exposed to a lot of different areas of the law, and decided to go in yet another direction. I practiced in some other areas and found that I was much better suited to representing individuals.

At first I represented individuals in all sorts of cases, from divorces to custody. I even served as a public defender for a number of years, representing kids who had been abused or neglected and subsequently removed from their homes. I found that to be very fulfilling.

As a public defender, I had some very difficult cases, including one in which a wife shot her husband after suffering years of abuse at his hands. She had met her husband years earlier, when she was picking cotton and he was in the US Army. She raised six kids, who lived all over the country and had very successful careers. They all came back to assist their mother with the difficulties she was experiencing in her later years.

The prosecutor wanted jail time, and her kids and I were adamant that jail would kill her. She had finally stood up to an abusive husband, and we believed she only fired the gun in self-defense. The forensic evidence was unclear. We had to try the case, and the jury determined that there wasn't enough evidence to find her guilty of murder but found her guilty of manslaughter. They didn't assess any jail time and fined her only $500. I will never forget my relief when they set her free. It was just one of those times when the law worked properly, but more importantly, a jury looked past the law and did what was right for the accused. That is the part of being a lawyer that I love: helping people in their time of need and doing what is right.

In that early part of my career I also represented a lot of low-income clients. I served as a branch president of my local congregation, a position similar to a bishop, and I ended up giving a lot of legal assistance to some of the struggling, poor members of my congregation. For the first eight or nine years of my career, I spent a lot of time representing people in criminal cases, abused kids in custody cases, and poor members of my congregation in whatever kind of case they needed help with. So most of my career to this point has involved representing those who have fewer resources and, usually, do not have the same access to justice as the wealthy might have or as corporations have.

While I still represent people in need—always an advocate of the underdog—my focus has been fine-tuned. In 2003 I was offered a job at a personal injury law firm. I took the job and primarily handled motor vehicle collisions, particularly many of the firm's tractor-trailer litigation and car wreck cases.

I had had a great deal of jury trial experience up to that point, and I had done some personal injury litigation on my own. One of the things I began understanding in that phase of my career was how significant an attorney's experience could be. I came to realize how perfectly suited my experience was to the work I was then doing. It was an eye-opening experience for me and significant in helping me realize how much value I could bring to clients.

Both motor vehicle and tractor-trailer litigation have become more specialized. When I first started practicing in the mid-1990s, almost every attorney, including myself, handled a few car wreck cases. But those cases became more difficult when tort reform changed the rules. Juries became tighter, and a lot of attorneys gave up their personal injury cases. To get fair results for your clients, you had to almost be a specialist in that area. So it became much more advantageous to restrict my work to motor vehicle collisions. Tractor-trailer collisions are even more of a specialized field, and that is what I primarily focus on today. A tractor-trailer collision is ten times more likely to be fatal than all other motor vehicle collisions, so naturally, the injuries are also likely to be more severe.

My professional interest in this type of case started at the personal injury firm, but my personal interest reaches back even further. Before I graduated from college, my sister was involved in a catastrophic car wreck, and it left a huge impression on me. She was driving with two of her friends when she turned into oncoming traffic and was hit head-on by another car. She and her two friends were airlifted to Little Rock for treatment.

The medical staff was not sure if any of them would make it, but all three of them pulled through despite having significant injuries. My sister had a traumatic brain injury, as did other passengers in the car. I saw firsthand how that collision affected them and continues to affect them even today. My sister still has some lingering problems, including headaches, as a result of the collision. A collision like that can be life changing, and this one certainly was for my sister.

My dad dealt with the defense attorney who was representing my sister against the other driver, and I remember my dad being adamant that all parties were adequately compensated and got what they deserved and that the results were just. It was clear to my dad that my sister had caused the wreck, and he did not want our attorney to hide anything. He wanted a fair judgment and fair compensation for everyone.

I am stunned by the number of times I have seen people who caused a wreck get defensive or act as if they are being taken advantage of by the other party. They are not willing to be accountable and to admit they caused the collision and should pay for the damages they caused. Seeing my father in action, dealing with the attorney representing my sister, showed me how a case should be handled. There was never any chance to minimize the damage or minimize what had happened. His concern, every time he spoke with the defense attorney, was to make sure that everybody was properly compensated. And that is what insurance is for.

My wife was also in a bad collision. When she was in high school, she was approaching a stoplight at an intersection when the light turned red. She stopped, but the tractor-trailer that was following her did not. It hit her from behind and sent her through the intersection. She ended up in a ditch all the way on the other side of the intersection. She hit her knee against the dashboard, and her car was totaled.

She went to the emergency room, where she was found to not have any broken bones. They released her the same day. The adjuster called my father-in-law a couple of days later in an attempt to resolve the claim. He offered to pay for the value of the car, minus the salvage, and for the hospital bills. But he told my father-in-law that Arkansas law did not allow any money for pain and suffering if a weight-bearing bone had not been broken. That is just not true. But it is exactly what he told my father-in-law.

My wife's family was not litigious. They just wanted to make sure that the legal outcome was reasonable. Unfortunately, they believed the adjuster. They assumed that what he was telling them was true, and they settled for the medical bills. They signed a release, settled the claim, paid the car off, and paid for the ER visit. Ten years later, my wife still had problems with her knee because it had never been properly treated, and the trucking company had not been held responsible. The trucking company never took responsibility for the damages or the medical care my wife needed later.

For years, when she and I were in a car, every time a tractor-trailer came up behind us, she would get nervous. We used to drive up to Fayetteville to visit her parents pretty regularly, and we had to take an old two-lane highway for part of the trip. A lot of tractor-trailers used that road, and every time we got on it, we would get into an argument or snap at each other, despite the fact that we were only on that part of the ride for about 30 or 45 minutes. Years later, we figured out why we had been arguing. It was because my wife was nervous and stressed about all of the tractor-trailer traffic. When they built an interstate all the way up there, we starting taking that road, and we argued less because there was more room for our car, and fewer tractor-trailers tailgated us.

Let me put this all into perspective. The interstate system we have in this country and the way we are able to move goods from coast-to-coast is invaluable, and tractor-trailers are a big part of that. The system benefits us all, and it has helped drive our economy. I do not want to end that. I do not have any axes to grind with regard to tractor-trailer drivers or companies. But anyone who is operating in that system and making a profit by shipping goods across state lines, or shipping goods on interstates, has a responsibility to be safe. If you are not held accountable when you are not safe, then being safe is not going to be a priority of yours. Holding people accountable makes them safer, plain and simple. What we lawyers do is not designed to hurt the trucking industry. It is designed to help the trucking industry and help the economy. All of us are better off when individuals and corporations are held accountable for the harms they cause.

My father-in-law drove a truck for many years, so I understand and appreciate all that truck drivers do. I know they have difficult jobs. I also know that, sometimes, they get pushed by their companies to drive longer hours, and they do not want to argue because that could mean losing their jobs. Often, it is not the truck drivers them-selves who are the worst offenders; it is the company they work for. Trucking companies may take shortcuts, get lazy, and make unrea-sonable demands on their drivers. The drivers do not want to get into a wreck any more than any of us do. They want to provide for their families. They want to be safe and be there for their families, just as we do.

So I think what I do helps all of us in that area. It keeps everyone safer. I feel very strongly about what I do, and in this book I am going to share my experiences and wisdom about tractor-trailer collisions and how to proceed once you have been involved in one. No one wants to get into a wreck. But worse than getting into a wreck is getting into a wreck and then not being treated fairly and not taking advantage of every opportunity available. I can help you with that.

Yes, you can represent yourself the whole way. This book will show you what I can do for you and what you can proactively do for yourself to get your case in the best shape possible. There are a lot of tools and techniques available to you, and I am going to lay some of them out for you in this book. This is my life's work, and being an advocate for the underdog is my guiding vision.

In early 2013, I opened my own law firm. I had been practicing law for a long time, and I felt I had something unique to offer. I had begun to get referrals from other attorneys who asked me for help with their complicated tractor-trailer collisions. So I felt it was time to strike out on my own, which is where I am today: available to help people in need, specifically people who have been involved in a tractor-trailer collision. Read on and learn how I can help you and how you can help yourself too. Put those two things together and we have the strongest case possible. That is my goal every time—for every one of my clients.

CHAPTER ONE

WHY TRUCKING CASES ARE DIFFERENT

We have a civil justice system because it is better than the alternatives. When somebody has caused harm, there are a number of things we, as society, can do. One, of course, is that we can criminalize the behavior of the accused and file charges against the accused. Another course of action is vigilante justice, in which people take the law into their own hands and right a wrong without government involvement. A third option, which we have used for hundreds of years, is our civil justice system. It is for actions that should not be criminalized, and it prevents vigilante justice, which can be arbitrary and violent. Quite simply, the civil justice system guarantees that all those who cause harm are held accountable.

If you break something, under the civil justice system you are responsible for fixing it. That is the basis of civil law. We try to correct wrongs and place a dollar amount on the harm that the wrongs have created. We try to make sure that the person who caused the harm pays the full value necessary to make the injured person whole again.

It is important to note that tractor-trailer collisions are different from all other motor vehicle collisions. When any kind of motor vehicle collision occurs, the negligent driver is accountable for the harms he or she has caused. Usually, a driver has insurance to cover damages, but having insurance coverage means the driver was taking responsibility in the first place. We want all drivers to have a financial stake in their own driving, as those with insurance coverage do. If we hold them accountable through the civil justice system and their insurance policy, they are more likely to be safe when they drive. It puts some skin in the game for them. We will get into more details about that in chapter two, but for now, we need to focus on the idea that those who drive negligently or poorly are responsible for the harms they cause and that tractor-trailer collisions are different from other types of motor vehicle collisions.

The first thing that sets them apart is the fact that a tractor-trailer and a car are vastly different in size and weight. Typically, a tractor-trailer is thousands of pounds heavier than a car. The average tractor-trailer is about 50,000 pounds compared to 6,000 for an SUV and 4,000 for an average car. When a tractor-trailer collides with an automobile, there is a much greater likelihood of damage to the car than there would be if a car collided with another car. The damage in the collision of a tractor-trailer with a car is likely to be more severe, and the injuries are usually going to be more severe. A tractor-trailer collision is ten times more likely to be fatal than all other motor vehicle collisions, so naturally, the injuries are also likely to be more severe. In my experience of handling these cases for the past 20 years, at least 40 percent of tractor-trailer drivers have been in violation of one of the safety guidelines.

There are a lot of ways in which tractor-trailer drivers can be negligent, and it is important to hold them responsible for every negligent act they commit or for failure to do everything they could have done to prevent the wreck. It is just as important to identify every individual or company that contributed in some way to the collision or failed to do something that could have minimized or prevented the damage. What you look for is anything others could have done that would have made everybody safer. Was there any valid reason for not taking that action?

We investigate multiple aspects of tractor-trailer wrecks because, often, the wreck was caused by a number of factors beyond the obvious. To begin with, tractor-trailer drivers and truck drivers are held to a higher standard than the average car driver. They are required to get a commercial driver's license, and that requires additional training in federal motor carrier safety regulations. The trucking companies, by the same token, are required to better train their drivers and make sure their drivers are doing everything possible to keep their trucks and the general public safe while they are behind the wheel.

We want to see the drivers' physicals. They are required to undergo a complete physical regularly so that we know they won't pass out and are safe enough to be behind the wheel of a tractor-trailer. It is not like the cockpit of an airplane where a copilot can take over if something goes wrong. The results can be just as devastating as an airplane problem, if not more so, if something goes wrong with the tractor-trailer driver.

It is stunning how often simple safety checks were not carried out on tractor-trailers that subsequently crashed—things that could have been fixed easily. Human error or judgment is not usually the cause of the collision, but rather, it is the driver's failure to make the simple, routine checks he should make every time he gets behind the wheel to make sure his truck is as safe as possible and he won't needlessly endanger the public.

These checks usually take only five or ten minutes before the driver gets behind the wheel of the truck. If drivers are not reminded regularly and the routine is not hammered into them every day at work, they start to cut corners. When one thing goes wrong, two or three things may also go wrong. If not addressed, a small problem that might not cause a collision or might simply alert the driver to pull off the road can develop into the cause of a collision or at least cause a lot more damage than it otherwise would have and even endanger life.

Let's return to the accountability of tractor-trailer drivers and how collisions with tractor-trailers are different. Say you have been hit by a tractor-trailer from behind. The thing most people immediately think of is that the tractor-trailer was either driving too fast or following too closely. In a lot of cases, one or both of those conditions is the cause of the collision and is easy to determine without a great deal of investigation. But with a tractor-trailer collision there are many other possibilities that also need to be explored. Were there things that could have been done days, weeks, or even hours earlier that would have prevented this wreck? Usually, there are a lot of these things.

Driver negligence is the most obvious cause of a wreck, but what are the things that lead to driver negligence? You want to look at all of the possibilities. We have identified the first type of negligence as whatever action the driver took or did not take at the moment of the wreck. Was there anything that was distracting the driver? Was he on his cell phone? Was he texting? Was he messing with his CB, or the radio, or doing something else? If the driver was taking some negligent action in the minutes before the wreck, he needs to be accountable for that. It is all part of holding him accountable and making sure that he is more careful in the future.

If we don't identify every area where a change could have been made that might have made the driving safer, we are not holding the driver or the trucking company fully accountable. If we find evidence of driver distraction in the driving records, the next thing to look at is driver fatigue. We want to know if the driver had been driving for such a long shift that his reaction time slowed. To determine this, we usually have to go back and look at the logbooks to see how long the driver had been on the road before the wreck happened. We may need to go back weeks to see what his regular schedule was. The Federal Motor Carrier Safety Administration (FMCSA) regulates the number of hours that a truck driver should be on the road. This is all outlined in the FMCSA Hours of Service regulations.

Drivers are required to keep logbooks showing every minute when they are driving and every minute when they are resting. They also have to log every minute when they are not driving but are still working for the company, which could be loading or unloading cargo or doing something else related to the trip. Such tasks involve neither driving nor rest. To determine driver fatigue, we cannot simply rely on the logbooks. We also need to obtain records of gas receipts showing when drivers stopped for gas and when they started driving again. Copies of any toll receipts, food receipts, expense sheets, and credit card statements could also give insight into how fatigued a driver was.

One case I had concerned a driver who had been driving from Oklahoma to Arkansas and was involved in a wreck in Arkansas. His logbook showed he had been driving for four hours just prior to the wreck. The interstate drive from Oklahoma City took about four hours. At first glance, there did not seem to be a fatigue issue. There was no evidence that he had driven too long or too far. However, when we requested the credit card receipts, the toll receipts, the food receipts, and the gas receipts, we learned some other things that were a little more interesting.

One was that he had, supposedly, taken an eight-hour rest immediately preceding his trip, in Oklahoma City. The wreck took place around 2 p.m. in Arkansas, a drive of approximately four hours from Oklahoma City. His logbook indicated that he had been resting from 1 a.m. until 10 a.m. that day in Oklahoma City, after which he drove from 10 a.m. until 2 p.m. before the wreck occurred.

Well, the toll booth receipts showed that he had paid a toll just about an hour's drive outside Oklahoma City, around 6 a.m., which was the time when, supposedly, he was resting. And a fuel receipt showed that he had fueled up in a spot west of Oklahoma City, also in that same time period between 1 a.m. and 10 a.m. So the logbook was not correct. The driver had not been resting from 1 a.m. until 10 a.m., as he had written in his logbook and reported to the government. He actually had been driving for about 12 hours straight just before he caused the wreck. So we have to look at driver fatigue, and we cannot simply rely on the logbooks for proof.

Logbooks are significant because they are only required to be kept for a certain amount of time before they can be destroyed. Depending on the severity of a wreck, the driver or trucking company may be required to keep a logbook longer. In any case, if we send out letters to the insurance companies and to the driver and his company asking them to retain this evidence, we may be able to keep it from being destroyed for a longer period of time.

The next thing we want to look at with regard to the driver is whether or not he was negligent in the repair, maintenance, and inspection of his truck. Drivers are required—again, by the Federal Motor Carrier Safety Administration—to inspect their trucks regularly. In fact, before every trip, the driver should carry out a pre-trip inspection of basic mechanisms in the truck. Drivers are supposed to conduct inspections thoroughly and mark down the results of those inspections.

In 2008 I had a case in which I represented the driver of a pickup truck who had met a dump truck head-on, on a dirt road in southern Arkansas. The pickup truck caught fire, and its driver died. He was burned so badly it was impossible to determine the cause of death. One thing that we discovered, among others, was that the dump truck driver had a fire extinguisher just underneath his seat, which he never pulled out and used, even as the pickup truck and its driver burned. When we looked at the inspection reports, we found that the fire extinguisher had not been inspected for more than two years. Had the truck driver been doing his inspections regularly, he might have been able to save that pickup truck driver's life.

Had the dump truck driver been doing regular inspections of the fire extinguisher, he would have been aware of where it was and probably would have been more likely to remember to grab it and use it and possibly save the other driver's life. Furthermore, if he had been carrying out regular inspections, the fire extinguisher would have operated properly, and he could have used it to rescue not only the pickup driver but also the three passengers in the pickup, of whom one survived and two died.

A good analogy here is the way a pilot inspects his aircraft before he flies. I have a close friend who is a pilot, and every time I used to fly with him in a little single-engine plane, I would get impatient because he seemed to take 15 minutes to complete the preflight check. He would go around looking at the wheels and the engine. He had this list of things he would check off, and he was very meticulous about checking all of them off. I quickly gained an appreciation for how important that inspection was, because if one thing goes wrong in a plane, especially if it is a single engine plane, everyone's life is in danger.

The same rule applies to the tractor-trailers. If something goes wrong with a tractor-trailer, lives are endangered: the lives of the general public who share the road with the tractor-trailers and who sit in vehicles that are, at best, one-fifth the size of a tractor-trailer. Every tractor-trailer driver should be properly trained and conduct a rigorous inspection before he gets behind the wheel to make sure that every part of his vehicle is operating safely every single time, including making sure his tires are inflated properly and there are no leaks, that his safety equipment is working, and, of course, that he is not tired. If all of those things were to be carried out by every truck driver, we could reduce the number of wrecks on the highway by a pretty significant margin.

Next, when we are investigating a collision, we want to know which actions the company took or did not take that could have made everyone on the road safer. The first principle is that truck companies are responsible for the actions of their drivers. That is generally the rule in every state, and Arkansas is no exception. The companies are responsible for all of the actions their drivers take. They are accountable, and they should be, just as the driver should be accountable. This means that the trucking companies have a responsibility to hire and train safe drivers.

The first thing we look at is whether or not the company was negligent in hiring that particular driver in the first place. Was this a driver who had a terrible driving record? Did he have 25 speeding tickets or previous driving under the influence charges or anything that would make most people say, "This guy should not be driving a tractor-trailer"? Should he be behind the wheel of one of those big trucks and endangering the public?

Did the company take reasonable steps to make sure that the person it hired is a safe driver? Did the company investigate the driver? We want to know if the driver had been involved in other collisions and what his prior employment was. I once had a case in which a truck driver was involved in a really bad wreck. He had been driving way over the speed limit, and he hit our clients.

One of the things we learned in discovery was that he had been fired from a previous trucking company for unsafe driving, and that company would not rehire him. The trucking company that subsequently did hire him, the one he was working for when our wreck happened, did not even make one phone call to inquire about the driving history or performance of this driver at his previous company. We know this because we obtained the company's phone records. Had the hiring staff called to inquire, they probably would have realized that this driver was unsafe, and they should not hire him to drive their trucks.

So to reiterate, the first thing we ask is whether the company was negligent when it hired the driver. Next, we ask whether the company properly trained or supervised its drivers. As we have already stated, a company is always responsible for the actions of its drivers. The company is making a profit by hiring drivers to transport goods across state lines, and so it has a responsibility to teach its drivers safe driving techniques and do all that it can to make sure its drivers are following safe driving techniques. Unfortunately, profits usually come first. They are usually valued above safety and accountability. Again, unless we hold a company's feet to the fire, that will always be the case.

Earlier in this chapter we discussed the driver with the logbook violations that he committed on his drive from Oklahoma City to Arkansas. The reality is that most companies have GPS devices in their trucks or have the ability to have GPS devices in their trucks. Even most cars have them these days. A GPS device would cost trucking companies about $100 per truck. But typically, trucking companies do not track the GPS data of their drivers, even if their trucks are equipped with GPS devices.

One obvious explanation for this is that they would rather bury their heads in the sand than know for sure when their drivers are speeding or when they are driving longer hours than required. In fact, in recent years, the National Transportation Board has recommended that GPS devices be put in every commercial vehicle over a certain weight, which would enable us to always be able to see where the truck was, how fast it was going, and where it was stopping. The trucking industry launched a massive protest against this recommendation, which still has not been mandated.

I have received a number of e-mails from associates who have represented smaller trucking companies. They claim the trucking companies would go out of business if they were required to buy and install these devices to track their drivers. We all know that these devices are not very expensive. I think everybody realized that it was not the cost of the device that was bothering all of these small trucking companies. It was the accountability that they did not like. So until trucking companies are required by law to use GPS devices, it is our responsibility to find out if the drivers involved in accidents were driving safely or if they were cutting corners and endangering the public.

Sometimes, truck drivers have their own GPS devices. They may have purchased the device on their own and placed it on their dashboard, or they may have a GPS feature on their phone. These are other sources of information we can use to help make our case stronger, especially if the device indicates an average speed or number of stops.

Another important question we like to find the answer to is whether the company properly trained its drivers in defensive driving. Every trucking company ought to offer regular safety classes to its drivers. When a company hires a driver it should be making sure not just that the driver passed his commercial driver's license manual test but also that he understands all aspects of it and is regularly being reminded of it. The challenge is that the manual has ten chapters. It is quite a bit bigger than a car driver's manual and not a manual that you could read one time and have it committed to memory. You need to go over it regularly, reviewing various aspects of it to make sure you understand how to handle a truck in certain situations and what types of dangerous circumstances you might find on the highway or as you approach an intersection.

In 1952 Harold Smith established the Smith System Driver Improvement Institute. Since then, the institute has trained millions of drivers on collision avoidance and defensive driving. It offers classes, videos, e-learning, and fleet monitoring to assist in making drivers better and safer. All commercial drivers should be exposed to this training, or similar training, but we find that in a large percentage of collision cases, the driver at fault has never been exposed to the Smith technique or any comparable safety training.

I once represented a man and his wife who were hit on Highway 71, just outside Mena, Arkansas. They had been pulling out from a stop sign and were hit broadside by a tractor-trailer on the highway. It was a tough case, and a number of attorneys had already turned it down on the assumption that the husband and wife were primarily responsible because they had pulled out into the path of the tractor-trailer.

Through our research we were able to find the tractor-trailer driver's cell phone records. This helped us track down GPS data and logbooks to determine how fast the driver was going immediately before the wreck. All of that helped in establishing some liability. Most disturbing in this case was the fact that the driver had been driving for this company for five years and had never undergone a defensive driving class during that time.

Most trucking companies employ a safety officer, or compliance officer, whose sole responsibility is to ensure the drivers drive safely. We interviewed this company's truck safety officer and learned that the company had not offered any defensive driving courses. One of the principles of Smith defensive driving is to not just to look in each direction before pulling out but to scan the road in each direction for a full 15 seconds. The industry standard, as listed in the Commercial Driver License (CDL) manual for Arkansas and J. J. Keller's Tractor-Trailer Driver Training Manual, is to look and scan for 12 to 15 seconds.

Another principle is that when a driver approaches an intersection, he should assume that other vehicles may pull into that intersection at the same time. In other words, a driver should identify all possible escape routes. He needs to have options so that he does not get boxed in when an emergency occurs. In our case, we used an expert safety officer to identify six different things that the truck driver could have done if he had been properly trained on defensive driving techniques to completely avoid the accident. First, he could have reduced his speed below the speed limit as he approached the intersection. He also could have surveyed the traffic and thought about the different options he would have in the eventuality of a dangerous situation. Had he kept a proper lookout and done all of those other things, he could have avoided the collision.

We made sure that we held each person accountable for the harms they committed. The driver of the car was certainly responsible for pulling out from a stop sign and into the path of an oncoming truck. But the truck driver was also accountable for driving too fast for the local road conditions, not keeping a proper lookout, and being fatigued because he had been driving for a longer period of time than he should have been. The trucking company was held responsible for not properly training the driver, for failing to make sure he knew the steps to take to avoid or minimize a collision. We would not have had much of a case had we not been able to fully develop all of the different areas of negligence that each driver was responsible for.

We can also check trucking company safety records. The US Department of Transportation's Federal Motor Carrier Safety Administration has a website that offers data about the safety history and accident history of trucking companies that have been at fault in wrecks: https:\\safer.fmcsa.dot.gov\. You can go there and get a snapshot of each company to find out how many wrecks its vehicles have been in over the last 18 months. You can view the company's whole inspection history, including whether or not company trucks failed any inspections and how many inspections they failed.

The site will tell you how many trucks the company currently has out on the road and how many other violations its drivers have had over that 18-month period as well. Every licensed commercial carrier's safety record is available at this site. Every commercial motor carrier is assigned a US Department of Transportation (DOT, or USDOT) number that is unique to that carrier and should be displayed on all their vehicles. This number serves as a unique identifier for the FMCSA to track the safety information mentioned above. You will need the company's DOT number to find their safety history on the website. The DOT number is easy to find. It is on virtually every police report involving a commercial carrier.

(Rev. 05/00)

ARKANSAS COMMERCIAL MOTOR VEHICLE COLLISION REPORT SUPPLEMENT

Page ____ of ____

Report # _____

Requirements For Use Of Commercial Motor Vehicle Supplement

A Commercial Motor Vehicle Supplement is *required* to be completed when the collision involves:

- A motor vehicle with a gross vehicle weight rating or a combination gross vehicle rating in excess of 10,000 pounds that is being used on a public highway to carry property; or
- A motor vehicle displaying a hazardous material placard; or
- A motor vehicle that is designed to transport 7 or more people including the driver;

AND

- The collision results in injury which requires the transportation of the injured person to a medical facility; or
- The collision results in a fatality; or
- Any vehicle involved in the collision is towed from the scene.

Sequence Of Events

1. Ran Off Roadway
2. Jackknife
3. Overturn (Rollover)
4. Downhill Runaway
5. Cargo Loss/Shift
6. Explosion/ Fire
7. Separation Of Units
8. Collision Involving Pedestrians
9. Collision With A Motor Vehicle In Transport
10. Collision With Parked Motor Vehicle
11. Collision With Train
12. Collision With Pedacycle
13. Collision With Animal
14. Collision With Fixed Object
15. Collision With Other Object
16. Collision With Work Zone Maintenance Equipment
17. Collision With Other Moveable Object
18. Collision With Unknown Moveable Object
19. Non-Collision
20. Non-Collision Equipment Failure
21. Non-Collision Other
22. Non-Collision Unknown
23. Other

Gross Vehicle Rating

☐ 10,001 To 26,000 Pounds   ☐ More Than 26,000 Pounds

Carrier's Identification Number

U.S. Dot # _____

ICC MC # _____

Carrier's Information

Name: _____

Address: _____

City: _____   State ____ Zip ____

Interstate Carrier? ☐ Yes ☐ No

☐ 1ˢᵗ ☐ 2ⁿᵈ ☐ 3ʳᵈ ☐ 4ᵗʰ

Hazardous Material

Did Vehicle Have A Haz Mat Placard? ☐ Yes ☐ No

Was There Hazardous Material Leakage? (Don't Count Fuel From Fuel Tank) ☐ Yes ☐ No

If The Vehicle Has A Placard Indicate The Following:

4-Digit Placard Number From Diamond Box   1-Digit Number From Bottom Of Diamond

Cargo Body Type

1A. Bus (Designated To Transport 7-15 People)
1B. Bus (Designated To Transport 16 Or More People)
2. Van/Enclosed Box
3. Cargo Tank
4. Flatbed
5. Dump
6. Concrete Mixer
7. Auto Transporter
8. Garbage/Refuse
9. Grain/Chips/Gravel
10. Pole
11. Not Applicable

Vehicle Configuration

1A. Bus (Seats 7 + People Including Driver)
1B. Bus (Seats 16 + People Including Driver)
2. Single Truck 2 Axle 6 Tires
3. Single Truck 3 Or More Axles
4. Truck/Trailer
5. Truck Tractor (Bobtail)
6. Tractor/Semi-Trailer
7. Tractor/Doubles
8. Tractor/Triples
9. Passenger Car (Haz Mat)
10. Light Truck (Haz Mat)
11. Unknown Heavy Truck

For collisions involving a tractor-trailer and a motor vehicle, the Arkansas State Police department requires additional paperwork to be completed, including the DOT number of the trucking company. And whenever there is a collision involving a tractor-trailer, the driver is required to take a drug and alcohol test within a short period of time following the wreck. The record of that test should be on the accident report as well. For a motor vehicle collision, some additional information will show up on the report, including the US DOT number, which is what you can use to find the company's safety record. There, you will find the rating of the vehicle. The report will also indicate if the tractor-trailer is under 10,000 pounds, between 10,000 and 26,000 pounds, or more than 26,000 pounds. You will also be able to determine if the tractor-trailer is an interstate carrier or an intrastate carrier, which may be important to your investigation.

As you can see, collisions involving 18-wheelers have much in common with motor vehicle collisions, but there are significant differences. Many differences are obvious, such as the greater likelihood of serious injury because of the size of the trucks. Other differences are less obvious but very important, so important that they actually change the way we conduct an investigation. In big truck cases, the defense usually has an accident reconstructionist, an investigator, and a very good attorney pulling their case together from the day of the wreck. There are pieces of evidence you need the insurance company to preserve, and there are questions about the trucking company that you need to review. There are things that each of us, including you—the injured party—can do, but we all work together as a team.

CHAPTER TWO

WHAT ARE THE CHANCES THAT MY CASE WILL GO BEFORE A JURY?

Frankly, if you have retained an experienced trial attorney, the chances that your case will go before a jury are slim. Insurance companies are more likely to settle your case and settle it for the full value of the claim if they know you have an experienced attorney who can take the case to trial if the case does not settle. In the past 20 years, I have tried more than 100 cases, and about half of those cases involved a jury. I have litigated several dozen cases in front of juries and deposed dozens of drivers, safety officers, trucking companies, truck safety experts, accident reconstruction experts, and police officers. Even through all of that, I still have to regularly refresh my knowledge of the commercial driver's license manual and the FMCSA guidelines. I have to make sure I am keeping up with it myself, so I know how important it is for trucking companies to give their drivers the same kind of training. I constantly refresh my knowledge of the old guidelines while also keeping myself up to date on the changes that come out periodically.

I have handled tractor-trailer cases in federal and state courts in both Arkansas and Texas. Some of those cases have involved the death of one or more parties in the collision. Others have been much less serious but still have caused long-term injuries and complications. I have tried cases that have involved a number of attorneys representing different interests and parties from multiple states. I have been brought in to assist other attorneys in their more complicated tractor-trailer cases. Over the past 20 years, I have obtained jury verdicts and settlements, totaling well over $40 million.

When you try a lot of cases, as I have, you build up a relationship with the important experts in the field. They are often just as important as the attorneys in the case because they can identify safety violations or other violations. I have great relationships with the people I consider to be the best experts in the area. I consult them and go up against them when other attorneys consult them. I am recognized by the National Association of Personal Injury Lawyers as one of the top ten personal injury trial attorneys in the state of Arkansas and by the National Trial Institute as one of the top 100 personal injury trial attorneys in the country. In other words, if you hire me as your attorney, your case will probably not go before a jury. That is a good thing.

What happens if you do not live in Arkansas but, unfortunately, are involved in a collision on an Arkansan roadway? Well, the law of Arkansas is going to determine the negligence of the parties. It is going to determine the law regarding the wreck itself. It will determine how much you are entitled to and the discovery required by both sides. It will affect most of the substantive issues involved in evaluating your case, and usually, you will be better off hiring a lawyer from Arkansas. It is not required that you hire an attorney from Arkansas or even any attorney, but I cannot think of many viable reasons to not hire a qualified attorney from Arkansas if you are involved in a wreck in Arkansas.

Of course, with the modern conveniences of telephones, faxes, e-mails, and other Internet communication, it is easy to be in contact with just about anyone, regardless of where that person is. It is less important to have an attorney who works in your geographical area than to have one who is experienced in tractor-trailer collisions and a specialist in these types of wrecks, specifically as they pertain to the law of Arkansas.

You will also probably want someone who works in the area of the collision site to take a look at the site and do some investigating. You want your attorney to be familiar with the scene of the collision, and that might be difficult to achieve if he is a few states away or even one state away. You will want an attorney who can talk to witnesses or have his staff talk to witnesses. You will want an attorney who knows the local experts and has a solid working relationship and history with them. Your attorney should know which experts perform best in front of juries and which ones are not so great when it comes down to courtroom performance.

Your opposition is guaranteed to hire a very good defense attorney, and it would help if your own attorney were somewhat familiar with the opposition's attorney or at least were to know something about the opposition's firm. You can find all of these qualities in a local attorney. It is always best to work with an attorney who would know the fine points of your case, from the scene of the collision to all of the players involved, and usually, that requires working with a local attorney.

I often tell prospective clients that if they have a minor case, if they are symptom-free, and if there is no significant damage to any of the vehicles involved, they can probably handle the case on their own. Living out of state would make this more difficult but not impossible. I also tell people to make sure that they are completely symptom-free because once they have settled a claim, they have settled it forever, and there is no going back and asking for more later, even if they later discover they have a significant injury.

That kind of client has come through my door. I had one who had been hit by a big truck. She did not think she was very hurt so she took a settlement for a few thousand dollars for her sore back, thinking the injury would resolve itself in a couple of days. She came to see me three months later. She had been to see her family doctor because the pain had not gone away. After undergoing an MRI, she learned that she had a herniated disk in her back, and she needed surgery to correct it.

Unfortunately, there was nothing I could do for her because she had already signed the release. She had already closed the case and agreed to take the $3,000 they offered her to compensate for the injuries to her back. Even in small cases you can handle on your own, you want to make sure you are completely symptom-free and have no lingering issues, because if you do and you settle, there is no going back.

CHAPTER THREE

THE FIRST 24 HOURS

Most of you who are reading this book are probably not reading it within 24 hours of your collision. But still, it is important for you to know what the other side was doing in those first 24 hours. If you happen to be lucky enough to be reading this within 24 hours of your collision—or even better, *before* your collision—you will benefit from some great strategies and tips you can employ to bolster your case. At the very least, you should do these things *as soon as possible*. There is no magic to "24 hours," but the sooner you take these steps, the better.

Because the first 24 hours are crucial for the trucking company and its attorney, they get very busy right away. Trucking litigation cases are very competitive for defense attorneys. Many defense attorneys want to handle trucking cases, so they work hard all of the time to impress their trucking company clients. Just as I do, the attorneys who represent trucking companies specialize in tractor-trailer litigation. Often, they travel from state to state trying their cases. I generally stay at home, so defense attorneys come up against me when I am in my own backyard, on my home field.

Trucking companies get in touch with their attorneys right away after a wreck, and there are a number of reasons they do that. One is that they can claim attorney-client privilege for a lot of things. In layman's terms this means they can be less than forthcoming with information. They obtain counsel early so they are fully prepared with every eventuality covered and the deck stacked in their favor.

They want to have someone evaluate the scene of the wreck immediately. They are mostly likely to hire an accident reconstruction expert to visit the scene and prepare a report for them. Of course, the experts will do everything with an eye to showing that the trucking company was not at fault or, at least, not totally at fault. Much of the time, the goal of the trucking companies is not to completely shed all liability, especially in clear-cut cases in which the fault of the truck driver is indisputable. But they always try to diminish their liability as much as possible. And they are ruthless.

Say, for instance, a tractor-trailer rear-ended a motor vehicle or crossed the center line and hit a car. You might think that the trucking company would not fight the litigation but, rather, admit it was at fault. That is often not the case. What a trucking company may do instead is try to find other liable parties to reduce its own liability. If it can show that 20 percent of the fault is that of the motor vehicle driver or somebody else, it will, eventually, pay a significantly reduced amount. So the trucking company will take all steps necessary to try to reduce its liability.

Arkansas is a state where the amount of liability reduces the amount that can be recovered. So, for example, if you had a case worth $1,000 and you were 25 percent at fault in causing the wreck and the trucking company was 75 percent at fault, the company would not owe you $1,000; it would owe you $750 or 75 percent of your total damages. When the figures are significantly higher, you can see why the company would look for every possible way to reduce its percentage of fault.

The company's investigators and experts not only look at the scene, take pictures, and identify evidence but also interview witnesses. They want to talk with everybody who was there and might have something to say that would bolster their case. Of course, when they interview witnesses, they try to lead them into giving as much information as possible to benefit the trucking company. They try to get a witness to say that the motor vehicle driver was driving too fast or not paying attention. They lead witnesses to talk about everything the motor vehicle driver was doing wrong. And the conversations will be recorded.

They will also download the electronic data from the tractor-trailer. Most of the engines now have at least one event recorder, if not more. They are similar to black boxes in airplanes but without voice recording capability. Event recorders can indicate the speed of a tractor-trailer prior to a sudden acceleration or sudden deceleration, going back anywhere from 5 to 30 seconds before impact.

If the truck also has a GPS system, it can indicate speeds that the trailer-tractor reached even further back in the moments leading up to the collision. Event recorders can also keep track of failures within the engine. The trucking companies' experts gather all of this information and much more very early on, sometimes even before the collision scene has been cleaned up. The truck driver probably will be required to submit to a blood-alcohol analysis, and that test is supposed to be administered by the police immediately.

As you can see, a lot of things happen right away on the side of the trucking company. But what about our side? What can we do to help our case? First, we can hire an accident reconstruction expert of our own. A good one can determine the speeds of both vehicles, the point of impact, and a lot of other evidence based on skid marks or gouges in the road. But a lot of these markings begin to disappear very shortly after the collision, which is one more reason to send an accident reconstruction expert to the scene as soon as possible.

That electronic data we discussed earlier? That goes away very quickly too—as soon as the tractor-trailer gets started up again. It is crucial to acquire that information immediately because as soon as someone turns the key in that truck's ignition, the electronic recorder resets itself.

The police and expert investigators are not the only people who can interview witnesses. This is one way you can help your own cause: by obtaining statements from witnesses. You can do it at the scene (if you are lucky enough to have read this book before your collision), or you can follow-up with people who saw the collision. Either way, it is important to talk to witnesses as soon as possible. We all know that memories fade, so the sooner you can get to witnesses, the better. Police reports will list the names of witnesses, but that does not mean those were the only witnesses to the wreck. If you know of others, talk to them. Share them with me and the rest of our legal team. We are all working together, and we love it when you do as much as you can to help our case. We will never ask you to do our work, of course, only the things that you can do and do well.

In those first 24 hours, the insurance company for the trucking company usually will have somebody contact you to take a statement about what happened. Be very careful about what you say or say nothing at all because by this point, you already will have given a statement to the police. The insurance company will be looking for inconsistencies in your statements or anything they can find to reduce the trucking company's fault and increase yours. You are not required to give a statement to the insurance adjusters early on, so your best bet is just to refer them to the police report. Do not let them trap you into saying something that they can use against you.

Pay very close attention to your injuries in the first 24 hours. You may receive medical care right away for obvious injuries, but if you have muscle or ligament damage, the pain may not show up until the next day when, suddenly, your body aches all over. So it is always crucial to seek medical attention immediately following a collision. Do not wait until something hurts. Go in and get X-rays and get checked out by a doctor, because medical staff can see problems that you do not even know exist. If you don't need to go to the ER, at least schedule a visit to your primary care physician for the next day or sometime in that next week. Just get checked out, and make sure to let your doctor know about every symptom—every single one—that makes you feel different from how you felt before the collision.

Even if you have been admitted to a hospital and released, you should follow up with your primary care doctor. There are two reasons for this: One is to make sure that you are healing properly and have been diagnosed properly. The other is that the defense lawyers will be looking at every possible reason to reduce the trucking company's liability and push the blame on you, and if there is a gap in your treatment, they can claim that you obviously were not hurt as badly as you had claimed. Also, it is important to document all of your injuries. Write them down. Keep a log of the things you cannot do as well or as efficiently since the collision occurred. Keep a record of how your injuries affect your day-to-day activities.

Head injuries are very important, obviously. We know a lot more about closed head injuries now than we knew in the past. We know that if you experience a concussion, even a minor concussion, it can lead to significant health consequences. We will delve into this later in the book, but the bottom line is that you must not withhold any information when you talk to your doctor. One injury can lead to another at a later date, and giving your doctor the most information possible is always the best practice. It is never easy to find a healed concussion. If you have even the slightest pain in your head, tell your doctor so that the proper tests can be conducted as soon as possible. Do not wait three or four weeks until you start getting regular headaches. At the first sign of pain, even slight pain, speak up.

Another important piece of advice is to not neglect minor injuries in favor of major injuries. Every injury is important, and some minor injuries can escalate. Make every single one of your injuries clearly known to a medical professional.

It is going to be months before your case settles, so make sure you get everything done as soon as possible—from your medical treatment to your witness interviews—so that nothing gets neglected or completely forgotten. In the same spirit, we want to make sure that we get everything we need from the defense as soon as possible. And whatever things we do not obtain right away, we want to make sure they save for us. We do that with a preservation letter, which requires them to provide certain information and evidence to us, even if they do not hand it over right away. I cannot stress enough how important this letter is. We send a copy to the trucking company, the driver, the insurance company, and the defense attorney. Some things that we request the trucking company hold for us include:

- Logbooks of the driver;
- All e-mails with regard to the driver and his trip that ended in his collision with you;
- Any photographs the driver may have taken. A lot of trucking companies put portable cameras in their trucks for drivers to use when they get into collisions. This way, the driver can document things if the investigator cannot get there right away. Some of these photos may be useful to our case, and if we do not ask them to save them, they will delete them. Drivers also use camera phones, and we want to obtain those photos too.
- All reports that the driver provided to his company, the police, some other investigating officer, or an accident reconstructionist;
- All receipts for fuel, food, tolls, and weigh stations;
- Expense sheets and any other documentation that might show where the driver was at a particular time;
- Event recorder data. The letter should state that the trucking company is not allowed to destroy the data or start the engine of the truck involved in the collision until the data has been downloaded.
- Copies of inspection reports of the truck for six months prior to the wreck and any inspection reports filed after the wreck;
- Repair and maintenance records of the truck for the year prior to the wreck;
- Photographs taken by the trucking company or one of their investigators, agents, or adjusters;

- The driver's personnel file, which shows all of his qualifications, moving violations, written tests, annual reviews, and physicals;
- All safety manuals and safety classes the trucking company has offered its driver, as well as the driver's attendance record, test results, and any other notes from his attendance in safety classes;
- All feedback the company received via the "How's my driving?" toll-free number it provided on the back of the truck.

Some cars have recorders just as trucks do, but you are not required to give a trucking company access to yours. It might be beneficial to have somebody interpret yours so you can see if it will help your case in any way, but you will never have to share that information with the other party.

One other thing to note about gathering information from witnesses is that the police do their best in a very short period of time after the accident, but they cannot be everywhere at once, and they were not involved in the collision. You can ask questions or obtain information from witnesses they would never even think to ask because you know the circumstances of the collision much better than they do. It is best to talk to witnesses right away, but remember that there is no time limit. You can talk to a witness right up until a trial, even while a trial is underway.

I had one case in which we thought all the witnesses had been interviewed, but we still could not resolve the liability issue, so we ended up filing suit. It was a case in which both drivers claimed they had a green traffic light. Additionally, each driver had exactly one passenger who confirmed the driver's story about having the green light. We were at a stalemate, and neither side would budge. About 15 months after the wreck we were in litigation, and we deposed one of the witnesses. We then learned of a third witness, whom nobody had previously identified. Shortly after the deposition, I made contact with the third witness, who had been in a different car at the time of the collision. He explained to me that he had stopped at a red light and had been passed on the left by a car that proceeded through the red light. After getting him to put his statement in writing, the case was resolved a few weeks later. It was a good example of how witnesses can be crucial to either side at any time during the case.

Everything we do is with the assumption that the case is going to go to a jury trial, so we always try to be as thorough as possible and follow every lead that might help our case. With that in mind, you should make a note of something that takes you two hours to do when it used to take you only an hour. You should photograph your injuries, even during their many stages of healing. Take as many pictures as you can take. Hundreds of pictures are not going to hurt you. Photograph the collision scene, your vehicle, and the truck. You cannot take too many pictures.

The last thing we need to do as soon as possible is coordinate your benefits. The insurance company and the medical providers and the hospital and the doctors all have a responsibility to help you—to either provide medical treatment or compensate you for that treatment. Unfortunately, they also have responsibilities to themselves involving profitability. That does not mean they cannot still serve you. It just means that they have goals that are different from yours.

Let's say you have MedPay coverage on your vehicle that provides $5,000 or more in medical benefits to be paid to you or your medical providers. They are usually no-fault benefits that can be paid regardless of who causes the wreck. You may also have health insurance. You have the right to receive benefits from both your medical insurance provider and your auto insurance MedPay policy. Coordinating your benefits will make sure that you receive all of the compensation that you are eligible for. You are in control of this, not the insurance companies. There are ways to get everything that is coming to you and pitfalls to avoid so that you do not miss out on anything. We can help with all of this, and we can show you ways to help yourself.

CHAPTER FOUR

THE FIRST TWO WEEKS

Without getting too bogged down with the literal schedule of things—the first 24 hours, the first two weeks—let me just say that the important thing is to start *now*. There is never really a reason to delay in the aftermath of a tractor-trailer wreck. You are probably wondering what things you can still do a week or two after your collision, and the good news is you can still do everything.

Continue to be diligent about your injury log, and if you have not started one yet, start it now! Log every little discomfort and inconvenience you are enduring because of injuries sustained in your collision. Continue to take photographs of your injuries. If someone is repairing your car, go and take pictures of that process. Show your car being taken apart and put back together again. Remember you can never have too many pictures.

But also remember this: keep your pictures and information to yourself. Be as antisocial about those things as possible. In other words, keep it all off social media. Do not mention a word or post a single picture about your collision on Facebook, Twitter, Instagram, or any other social media platform. Do you know why? The defense is watching you. Do not think that your privacy settings will keep them out. They will go so far as to friend your friends in order to get access to your data. Yes, they are monitoring all of your accounts and just waiting for you to say or show something they can use in their favor. I usually monitor their social media accounts on your behalf as well, and I almost always find something useful when I do.

Keep your log private. Write things down in a spiral notebook, and document everything that you cannot do, and assume that someday, we will present this information to a jury. Do not talk about how much pain you are in, because that is an abstract concept, and a jury cannot feel your pain. Follow the advice of Joe Friday in Dragnet and give them "just the facts." Talk about things that you can no longer do because of your injuries. They can relate to that. Everyone can. They can appreciate your having to miss work because you cannot get in and out of your car or your difficulty in walking more than 100 yards. They can relate to the fact that you cannot mow your lawn or that it takes three times longer to wash the dishes because of an injury you sustained in your collision. Tell them how your sleep patterns have been disrupted and how that affects all other areas of your life. Document all of it as it is happening. Do not give your memory time to fade.

Coordination of benefits is important during this time, and it is something I see my clients mishandle in 95 percent of my cases. The mistakes are always made before an attorney is involved, so perhaps it is worth mentioning that seeking the counsel of a qualified attorney as early as possible is just as important as any of these other steps.

Arkansas is a "made-whole" state, which means the ultimate goal is to fully and adequately compensate the injured party. That goal trumps the right of other insurance companies to be reimbursed for claims they have paid. It means that injured parties have greater rights, and proper coordination of benefits is very important. The made-whole law recognizes that you are the only person in the case who did not come in voluntarily, and your rights trump those of the insurance companies and even the medical providers.

Most Arkansas medical policies carry no-fault MedPay insurance or personal injury protection (PIP) insurance. In fact, your insurance company is required to offer it to you in a minimum amount of $5,000. If you do not wish to carry that coverage, you are obligated to waive it in writing. In Arkansas, if you have not waived your right to buy PIP or MedPay insurance, you are deemed to have it, and you still have that $5,000 MedPay benefit. Often, the medical providers make their claims for the first $5,000 of medical treatment directly to these MedPay providers. That $5,000 can be spent very quickly on hospital bills and radiologists and ER doctors and other physicians who see you in those first few weeks after the wreck.

If you have health insurance, it is important that you first use your health insurance to pay these bills, and then use your MedPay insurance for deductibles and copayments. If you do it that way, you can stretch your dollars considerably and make sure that you have enough to pay all of these bills upfront without having to wait for the settlement with the trucking company.

The reason this is important to do is twofold: 1) you do not want to add the stress of receiving collection notices and having hospitals call you to get the rest of their payment, 2) you do not want the threat of bill collection affecting your negotiating position with the trucking company for the final resolution of the case. It is never a good idea to settle your claim with a trucking company until you know exactly how badly you have been injured and how long that injury will last.

If the insurance company feels you are in a hurry to settle the case, it is more likely to try to lowball you and offer you less than the real value of the case. It will assume that it has negotiating leverage because you want to take what you can get and resolve the case as quickly as possible. This is never a good position to put yourself in. Be patient and let your attorney help you properly coordinate your benefits. Meanwhile, you should contact all of your insurance companies and make sure they know about the wreck. This too will make coordinating your benefits easier.

Another thing you can do in the first couple of weeks is have your car appraised. If you have an insurance company, it is probably already doing that, and if you are comfortable leaving it up to your insurance company, fine. But have someone look at your vehicle before anything changes. Even if it is totaled, have someone look at it. Have someone officially deem it "totaled." During repairs, you are entitled to have the trucking company provide a rental car for you. If your car is totaled, you are entitled to a rental car until you have been paid the fair amount for your car. Do not delay getting your car appraised because if you don't, it will only hurt you in the end.

If you have not already downloaded the event recorder data from your own car, do it in the first two weeks. Do it before you restart your car because the recorder may reset as soon as you turn your ignition key, as it does in trucks. Find someone you can trust to download the data for you so you can see whether it is useful to your case or not and so you can make sure that it has not been corrupted or modified.

In the first two weeks, the truck driver needs to be investigated. For this, you almost always need an attorney or a private investigator. As your attorney, I will find everything I can find out about him: his driving record, his history, the things we cannot access right away, or the things that a truck driver could conceal in some way—it will all be listed in the preservation letter.

An extreme example of this would be a prior conviction for a drug offense or some other conviction that the truck driver could have expunged or sealed. If he had been thinking about getting it expunged or sealed, he might think about doing so a lot more quickly after he gets in a wreck.

One thing you can find out is how safe the trucking company is and what sort of safety environment it fosters among its drivers. Find out how much the company invests in safety classes and safety training. Find out how often it gives its drivers safety instructions, refresher courses, and safety certifications above and beyond the bare minimum that the federal government requires of commercial drivers.

Whenever we get a new case, one of the things we check in the first 72 hours is the company's safety record measured against other trucking companies. I want to know how good or bad the trucking company is at following the rules. If the company has more safety violations than 75 percent of the companies out there, I know I will be dealing with a company that does not want its safety record to be put in front of a jury and will be more likely to settle for full value.

Make sure to follow up with your doctors so that the defense cannot say that your injuries were not as bad as you made them out to be. Just be safe and get your follow-up care. Do not show the defense any gaps in treatment. They will then not be able to use that against you. Besides the defense claiming your injuries could not be as bad as you indicated, they could also argue that because of your gap in treatment, your injuries could have been sustained after, and completely unrelated to, the collision. Do not give them that opportunity. It is, of course, very important that you do not exaggerate your injury, but it is also just as important that you do not minimize it. Just state the facts in your logbook, and you will be fine.

If your collision occurred in a construction zone, it may be important to have overhead photographs taken in the first two weeks following the collision. We do this so we can later recreate the scene to ensure there is no question as to how the accident happened. Overhead shots are not as expensive as they might seem, and they are almost always worth the trouble.

CHAPTER FIVE

COMMON CAUSES OF TRUCK COLLISIONS

The time it takes for tractor-trailers to slow down to a stop is a lot longer than for most road vehicles. Drivers should be aware of everything that could be in their path that they would not be able to avoid in the next 15 seconds. Tractor-trailers often have blind spots that can cause major problems. Turns can be challenging at times, and drivers should always exercise caution when going around corners or curves of any kind. Wide-right turns and U-turns can be particularly dangerous.

Talking on a cell phone in an automobile is dangerous. It is even more dangerous when the driver of a 50,000-pound tractor-trailer talks on a cell phone. Texting is worse still. Tractor-trailer drivers are never supposed to use cell phones when they are driving, but some of them do, and they end up in collisions because of it. A hands-free cell device is no solution. If drivers are talking, their mind is distracted. It is not just about clear vision and free hands. It is also about attention and focus.

If the tractor-trailer driver's company taught the Smith defensive driving method, the driver would always be alert to potential dangers, including anticipating other drivers' dangerous actions and reactions.

DON'T FORGET YOUR KEYS!

1) AIM HIGH IN STEERING.
2) GET THE BIG PICTURE.
3) KEEP YOUR EYES MOVING.
4) LEAVE YOURSELF AN OUT.
5) MAKE SURE THEY SEE YOU.

Maintaining this constant state of alertness would be nearly impossible if the truck driver were using a cell phone. As I mentioned in an earlier chapter, a few years ago I handled a case involving a husband and wife who were trying to enter a busy state highway from a side road. They made a left turn, and a tractor-trailer hit them broadside. No attorney wanted to take their case because they pulled out directly into the path of the truck. I ended up representing the wife, who was the passenger in that vehicle.

Under Arkansan law, since she was not at fault, it did not matter much how much at fault her husband was. She was able to recover the percentage of her damages attributable to the tractor-trailer driver and potentially, against her husband as well. Basically, we had to determine which percentage of the wreck was the fault of her husband and which percentage was the fault of the tractor-trailer driver.

She had sustained pretty extensive injuries, and we were trying to pursue a claim against the tractor-trailer driver and the trucking company. One early claim made by my client and her husband was that the truck had been going faster than it should have been and was coming over a rise, so it was not completely visible until it was too late. There were only about 200 yards between the top of the rise and the intersection. The case went into litigation, and when we subpoenaed the phone records, we found that the driver of the tractor-trailer had been talking on a cell phone right before the collision. One of the principles of the defensive driving manual is that drivers at intersections should anticipate the approach of vehicles coming from the other directions. So while the husband had the responsibility of not pulling out in front of the truck, the truck driver also had a responsibility of preparing for what would happen if someone did. There is no way he could have done that while talking on a cell phone.

The truck driver did not change his course even though there was a turn lane, and he had intended to turn left. He could have taken an alternative path and avoided impact. But he did not because he was talking on his cell phone and not paying attention to the road and its many hazards. We downloaded the electronic data from the truck and determined that he also had been speeding. When we deposed the truck safety officer, we learned that the trucking company had never given this driver Smith defensive driving training or any other significant defensive driving classes. He had enough training to pass the commercial driver's manual test and get his commercial driver's license, but he had no training beyond that. Having no chance of winning in a trial, the trucking company settled out of court with us.

Radios and CBs are another form of distraction for truck drivers. Nothing good happens when a driver is fiddling with one of those. They are pure distraction. Beyond that, they require drivers to remove their hands from the steering wheel or gear shift. What good can come out of that? A lot of drivers these days listen to satellite radio, and often there is a record of what they were listening to at the time of the collision. Was the program they were listening to particularly distracting? This is something we need to find out, especially if it will help our case.

Quite simply, speeding is probably the most common cause of truck collisions. Speed is probably the tractor-trailer's worst enemy. Trucking companies that care about safety and train their drivers to be safe and not endanger the public should encourage their drivers to keep their speed below the posted limit. After all, that limit was designed for automobiles and smaller trucks, which can slow down and change direction much more quickly and easily than tractor-trailers can. Any good safety director will tell drivers that if they approach a curve where the speed limit is 45 miles per hour, they need to drive 10 miles per hour below that limit, because negotiating the curve will be trickier for them than for the drivers of smaller vehicles.

Some trucks have governors on them, which goes back, again, to how seriously a company takes driver safety. There is a huge gap between the safest companies and the most dangerous companies on the roads today. The US Department of Transportation tries to monitor and punish companies that do not take driver safety seriously. But a speeding fine of $200 from the transportation department or a police officer does not make a trucking company accountable, considering how much they make in profit and how much more they make when they get goods delivered more quickly than usual.

The only way to make trucking companies accountable and keep their drivers operating safely is to hit them where it matters: in their pocketbooks. Lawyers have to make sure they hold them accountable for everything they do wrong to eliminate any incentive they might have to overlook driving safety precautions.

Construction zones are also a pretty significant cause of collisions. One case I had in Texas involved a tractor-trailer colliding with a pickup truck. The tractor-trailer driver had maintained all along that he was driving under the speed limit. It was a construction zone, but the speed limit did not change. It was still set at 45 miles per hour through the intersection where the construction was taking place. However, a danger sign, placed about 300 yards before the intersection, recommended that drivers reduce their speed to 30 miles per hour. This sign was not identified in the police report, but we went out and took pictures of it. The truck driver's speed, based on the electronic event recorder, was 45 miles an hour.

He was driving at the speed limit, which was actually 15 miles per hour faster than the recommended speed. Again, if he had had good safety training, he would have known that he should have been traveling below 30 miles an hour. He should have been driving at about 25 miles per hour as he approached the intersection. Not only are speeds lower in construction zones, but lanes are often narrower too, and that makes a difference for tractor-trailers. Because of the trailer-tractors' larger size and their blind spots, when cars get bunched up in those tight spaces, they can disappear from view of the truck driver. Furthermore, besides the regular traffic moving through the construction zone, construction vehicle traffic often operates there too. Tractor-trailer drivers always need to be on the lookout for slow-moving construction vehicles pulling into traffic in construction zones.

Especially in inclement weather and at night, it is important for a tractor-trailer's lights and reflectors to be in good working order. Any parts of them not visible because of missing lights or reflectors can cause huge problems for other motorists.

Since 1967, trucking companies have been required to install what is often called a Mansfield bar at the rear of their trailers.

The bar is a guardrail that stops a car from going all the way under a trailer, the underside of which is much higher than a car's hood. These bars are named for the actress Jayne Mansfield, who was killed when the car she was in slid underneath a tractor-trailer. Hopefully, one day soon, when all tractor-trailers have that bar, that kind of wreck will be a thing of the past. The bars are required by law, so any truck traveling without one is in violation of the law. Even though most trailers have some type of underride protection, like the Mansfield bar, there are still design defects that could be easily improved for greater safety. Many of them are too narrow, not extending adequately to each side of the trailer. Others are too far off the ground to be effective for smaller cars. And still others are not sufficiently strong to prevent many cars from breaking them and still going under the trailer. Anyone involved in a collision with the underside of a trailer should have the trailer inspected to ensure it is in compliance with FMCSA regulations and properly designed.

There is a similar bar that serves the same purpose along the sides of trailers. These are not yet required by law, but if everyone were to use them, we could prevent a lot of wrecks involving cars sliding underneath trailers from the side. The National Transportation Safety Board issued a recommendation in April 2014 asking the National Highway Traffic Safety Administration (NHTSA) to require side under-ride protection systems on all new trailers. It will be a great day when this safety measure becomes mandatory, as 15 percent of fatal tractor-trailer collisions are due to side-impact collisions.

It should go without saying that fatigue is a huge cause of tractor-trailer wrecks. The US Department of Transportation has detailed rules and regulations about how long drivers should drive and how long they should rest, but not everyone follows those guidelines. The hours vary depending on whether the drivers are traveling across state lines or not, but generally, if drivers adhere to the guidelines, they should be adequately rested and alert while driving. There are "per-day," "per-week," and "per-trip" hours, and all drivers—and trucking companies—should pay attention to them.

But the fact is a large percentage of trucking companies have, historically, objected to the hours of service requirements. They think the regulations create an unreasonable burden on them and significantly cut into their profit margins. Their incentive is to get their materials out as quickly as possible and delivered as quickly as possible so their guys can deliver something else as quickly as possible. Every hour that a tractor-trailer spends sitting on the side of the road or in a warehouse makes no money for trucking companies. So they have an incentive to get their trucks on the road as much as possible. That makes for some very tired drivers.

Just because drivers say they are in compliance with their logbook does not mean they are. We verify this by comparing the logbook to parking tickets and charges for tolls, fuel, food, and other things. We can compare all of those things, side by side, to get to the truth. It is, unfortunately, very common for truck drivers to manipulate the numbers in their logbooks so they appear to be in compliance, even when they drive for longer periods of time than allowed. If the trucking industry had provided their drivers with electronic logbooks linked to GPS systems in the early 2000s, manipulated records would not even be an issue today. This improvement has still not been made, and the industry opposes it, which is a clear indication that many trucking companies and drivers are still fudging the numbers in their logbooks to best suit their needs.

Many trucking companies and drivers cut corners or hit the road not properly prepared, and all of these things can lead to wrecks with unsuspecting, innocent motorists among the general public.

CHAPTER SIX

ELEVEN QUESTIONS TO ASK YOUR ATTORNEY

1. WHAT ARE MY CHANCES OF GOING TO TRIAL?

Nobody really wants to go to trial. Most clients would prefer to have a case resolved without having to go through the stress or the time commitment of a jury trial. Yet many of those people falsely believe that if they hire an attorney, they will have to go to trial and face a jury. The truth is the odds of going to trial *decrease* when an experienced attorney is hired early in the process.

The most significant factor in determining whether or not you have to go to trial is how sufficiently prepared you are for trial. If you are sufficiently prepared, your chances of going in front of a jury go down significantly. When you have a competent attorney on your side, you will be sufficiently prepared for trial.

Only about 20 percent of most traffic collision cases I handle move to litigation, and about 10 percent of those that move to litigation actually go to trial. So a relatively tiny number of cases—about 2 percent of all cases—make it to trial. This percentage is slightly higher in tractor-trailer-specific cases, but it is still quite low.

2. HOW MANY CASES HAVE YOU TRIED?

It is important to ask any attorney you consider hiring how many cases he or she has tried before a jury. You may also ask how many cases that attorney has tried before a judge. Many attorneys have tried hundreds of cases before judges but may not have tried a single case in front of a jury. A trial in front of a jury is significantly different from a bench trial (a trial before a judge). Trials before judges can include custody hearings, bankruptcy hearings, misdemeanor traffic violations, and all sorts of other such cases. Experience in trying cases before a judge does not necessarily qualify an attorney to represent you in a tractor-trailer case before a jury—or even before a judge, for that matter. Only work with an attorney who has tried several tractor-trailer cases in front of both juries and judges.

It is extremely rare for a tractor-trailer case to be heard just in front of a judge and not in front of a jury. But again, only about 20 percent of our tractor-trailer cases enter into litigation, and that usually results in a handful of trials per year. Most firms also have websites that list their verdicts and settlements. Make sure to take a look at them.

I have tried more than 100 cases, so I have experience with juries, defense attorneys, and the expert witnesses that both sides use.

3. HOW MUCH WILL THIS COST ME?

Typically, attorneys handle personal injury cases on a contingency basis. That usually means the victim is not responsible for any of the attorney's fees unless a positive outcome is reached. Virtually all tractor-trailer cases should be handled on a contingency basis. It minimizes the risk to you, and it also aligns your interests with the attorney's interests so that when your attorney benefits, you benefit, and vice versa.

In tractor-trailer cases, a common contingency fee arrangement is between 33 percent and 50 percent of the total settlement. That means that one-third to one-half of the settlement goes to the attorney, and the rest goes to the client. Talk to your attorney about the expenses he might incur. Attorneys handle this in different ways, and you need to make sure you understand not only how the contingency fee agreement works but also how the expenses agreement works.

Many attorneys front the cost of litigation on their own, and your attorney should be willing to do that. The attorney will hire all of the experts needed to make your case, which can get expensive. As long as he covers those costs on the front end, you are fine. Money will never leave your pocket. Instead, you will get your share of the settlement, minus costs, when the case is resolved. Just as important, you should discuss with your attorney how those expenses would be handled if your case were to prove unsuccessful. Some attorneys swallow the costs, and others charge them back to the client. Make sure you know what you are getting into.

4. WHAT IS MY CASE WORTH?

I will go into more detail about the value of a case in chapter eight, but it is important to know that the value of your case has a number of variables attached to it. In Arkansas you are entitled to the total cost of your past medical expenses as well as the total cost of the medical expenses you may reasonably be expected to incur in the future. You are also entitled to an amount for the pain, suffering, and mental anguish you suffered as a result of the injuries. You are entitled to compensation for the nature, extent, and duration of the injury, including whether or not that injury is permanent or temporary.

You are also entitled to the gross value of any wages you lost as a result of your injury and may be entitled to claim expenses for health care and nursing should you need to hire someone to help you with activities you can no longer perform—for example, house chores. You are entitled to compensation for scarring. Those are the first things you look at in determining the value of your case. But remember that tractor-trailer collisions are litigated differently from car collisions. This is partly due to the fact that case values are determined by the other side's behavior.

Juries understand that it is important to hold tractor-trailer drivers and their companies accountable for the harms they have caused and for their negligence. Knowing the extent of the defendant's unsafe activities helps us narrow down what the true value of your case might be.

5. WILL HIRING AN ATTORNEY ADD VALUE TO MY CASE?

Another way to ask this is "Won't hiring an attorney just take money out of my settlement?" That is a valid concern, and you need to be comfortable with the idea of hiring an attorney. It is also an issue that an insurance company adjuster will remind you of because he will want you to settle your case before you hire an attorney.

In fact, when adjusters make an offer or try to settle a case before an attorney is involved, one of the most common things they tell claimants is, "If you don't take my offer, you'll end up with less money because your attorney will just take a percentage of it." This should clue you in to the fact that the adjuster is already selling you short. He is banking on the belief that you will take a smaller settlement to avoid forfeiting some of your settlement to attorney's fees. However, hiring an attorney usually results in a better offer from the insurance company.

It does you no good to hire an attorney who increases the case value by 10 percent but takes a 33 percent fee because then you have lost 20 percent. It is important to talk to your prospective attorney about how he or she might add value and by how much. Ask if the value he or she expects to add will increase your bottom line. Ask how the attorney will do it—through expert witnesses or through coordination of your benefits? Ask for specifics.

In my experience, attorneys add much more value than they take in fees if they are familiar with and experienced in tractor-trailer cases. I would say, on average, attorneys add two or three times the value cases would have had without their involvement. That is a net benefit to you.

6. CAN I SEE SOME REFERENCES FROM PAST CLIENTS, AND CAN I TALK TO THOSE CLIENTS?

In my case, absolutely. All reputable attorneys will have references for you to consider, and if they do not, you should stop considering their services right then and there. I have reviews from past clients on Avvo.com, Lawyers.com, and even on a Facebook page.

AVVO.COM REVIEWS:

Posted by Jim, a trucking accident client, four years ago:

I recommend Alan, who handled my trucking accident case. I have previously worked with three to five lawyers. Alan was very professional in looking out for my interest and spent countless hours to get me the best settlement I could have hoped for. I would request him again if I had to go through this process.

Posted by Brian, an attorney in Little Rock, Arkansas, almost four years ago:

I endorse this lawyer. Having handled a number of cases against Alan LeVar, I've learned that behind his calm demeanor and understated style is a first-class legal mind. The fact that he is willing to fight for his clients is evident by his careful attention to each case. I also know firsthand that many lawyers seek Alan LeVar's advice when they are confronting novel legal issues. His intellect and hard-working style ensure excellent guidance.

Posted by Michael, a military law attorney in Evans, Georgia, five months ago:

I endorse Alan. He is a highly skilled attorney who is well respected in the legal community.

Posted by Natalie:

Working with Alan makes normally very stressful situations practically stress-free for me. He comes across as a very caring, honest, and diplomatic individual.

FROM LAWYERS.COM:

I have used Alan's services twice now for family auto accidents. I can say I highly recommend him. He has done an outstanding job, and we received more than fair settlements. Alan is very honest and straight with you about your case, and he has gone over and above for us, even helping with an unrelated legal matter that he didn't charge for, as a favor to me. Now, I consider him a friend of the family. Never saw that coming out of an auto accident. Thanks, Alan!

FROM FACEBOOK:

Kristen—5 stars:

Alan is a great guy! Have known him since grade school. He will protect your rights and serve you well as your lawyer. He has ethics that most lawyers can't boast about. Your case will be in great hands with Alan.

Corey—5 stars:

I've known Alan for over 25 years. Alan is one of the best guys I have ever met. He's honest, sincere, and dedicated to his profession.

Melissa—5 stars:

> Mr. LeVar was my divorce attorney back in 2002. He was great.

Pat—5 stars:

> I have known Alan LeVar since he was a top student in my biology class in the tenth grade. He has been a close family friend ever since. I know no better man, a man you can fully trust and depend on.

I make sure to talk to prior clients of mine about their representation and ask them how it went. They are usually very satisfied, and they want to tell me so or write a public letter declaring how satisfied they were with my services. I encourage my prospective clients to read my reviews and references so that we can go into our case feeling comfortable about each other and knowing what to expect. My referrals certainly help me attract new clients. I am proud of them, and I welcome anyone to read them. I am also happy to connect prospective clients with past clients for live conversations. It is important to speak with past clients of the attorney you are considering to represent you in your case. You also should Google your attorney's name just to see what else is out there. By Googling the attorney, you can find out if any complaints about him were lodged with the Arkansas Office of the Committee on Professional Conduct.

7. HOW OFTEN WILL I HEAR FROM YOU OR SOMEONE IN YOUR OFFICE?

Communication is vital to making sure your case is moving along promptly and that all of your issues are being addressed by the attorney. Regular communication also lets you know whether the attorney has enough time to spend on your case and is giving your case sufficient attention.

Even while you are talking to a doctor or are undergoing medical treatment, you should have regular communication with your attorney—at least once every couple of weeks. In our office, it is a requirement that staff have contact with every client every couple of weeks. Even if we cannot proceed with anything—for example, our client may be recovering from surgery and not able to communicate—we still want assure our client that we are aware of everything, that nothing is being overlooked, and that all details are being covered.

Some attorneys do not always use the telephone. They might send you an e-mail or even a letter in the mail. You should know not only how often your attorney wants to communicate with you but also how often your attorney will initiate that contact. You should not have to track your attorney down. Your attorney should keep you apprised of every new development in your case.

8. PROCEDURALLY, DO I EVEN NEED AN ATTORNEY?

There are a number of things you can do on your own to make sure that your case is being handled appropriately and to make sure that everybody on your side is working to prevent everybody on the other side from working against you. The first thing you can do is coordinate your benefits.

When you are in a wreck, you have access to a number of different insurance companies that should provide you with benefits. The most obvious one is the insurance company of the tractor-trailer that hit you. You probably also have insurance on your vehicle, which may include coverage of no-fault medical payments. And if you have health insurance, you have also been paying for that benefit. It all needs to be coordinated, and you can start that process by just talking to your insurance companies and telling them about your wreck.

Very soon this will all get complicated, and that is when it is best to have an attorney handle it for you. Remember that insurance companies hire the best defense attorneys to represent them in trucking cases. The competition is fierce among defense attorneys vying for these cases because they are quite profitable. What this means is every effort you put forth is countered by the insurance companies. They have their best attorneys gathering evidence and doing their best to minimize their liability. When they speak to you, they look for things they can use later to minimize your claim—and those conversations are always recorded. It is always best to have an attorney speaking for you and helping you through some of the more complex processes in your case.

9. DO YOU HAVE THE TIME TO WORK ON MY CASE?

Some attorneys spend a lot of time trying to sign up clients but do nothing with their cases. They let them sit for 12 or 18 months and file lawsuits just before the statute of limitations runs out. Some attorneys take on cases, spend a lot of time advertising those cases, and then expect the insurance company to make them offers. Neither of those scenarios is any good for you.

You want an attorney who has time to work on your case from the very beginning to the very end. It is about putting in the time, but it is also about assembling a great team that will allow your attorney to do everything he or she needs to do to represent you and make sure all avenues are covered. With that in mind, do not forget to ask about your attorney's team and resources.

Most good attorneys will have at least one case manager and a paralegal assigned to every case to make sure that all issues are being developed, all evidence is being gathered, and all medical records are put together. They will also make sure that chronologies are created and any future medical treatment is anticipated. Tractor-trailer cases take time and require a lot of resources. Make sure your attorney is up to the task before you hire him or her.

At our offices, we take pride in keeping our attorney-to-client ratios low, our staff-to-client ratios low, and in making sure all our clients get the proactive attention they deserve. Many of our clients compliment us on the amount of time we spend regularly updating them on the progress of their cases or checking up with them while they complete medical treatment.

10. HOW LONG WILL THIS TAKE?

I understand the desire to resolve things as soon as possible, but the first thing I caution clients about is settling their case before their medical issues have been fully resolved. Once you settle a case, you settle it forever, and there is no going back.

It is important you make resolving your medical issues your number-one priority. Your job, as the plaintiff, is to make sure you receive the proper medical care you need—all of the medical care you need. Only you know how you feel. Do not rush through your treatment, and do not try to act tough. Get the care you need, and get your body and mind back to where they were before the wreck. Let your attorney work through the legal aspects of the case while you get the proper care for your body. Pay attention to your symptoms and monitor them through the whole process. It takes as long as it takes. Only when you feel right, when you feel that you are back to your whole self, is it time to settle.

I usually tell clients they may be in a position to begin discussing the value of their settlement four to six weeks after they finish medical treatment. If an agreement can be reached, a case can be settled a week or so later. But the time leading up to the settlement takes as long as it takes and should never be rushed, not even a little.

11. IF I WERE IN A WRECK IN ARKANSAS, BUT I DIDN'T LIVE THERE, WOULD I NEED AN ARKANSAS ATTORNEY?

If you are involved in a wreck in Arkansas and you live in, say, Illinois, the law of Arkansas will determine the negligence of the parties. It will determine the law regarding the wreck itself. It will also determine how much you are entitled to and the discovery required by both sides. So the law of Arkansas will affect most of the substantive issues involved in evaluating your case, and usually, you will be better off having a lawyer from Arkansas represent you if your wreck occurred in Arkansas. It is not required that you hire an Arkansan attorney—or any attorney for that matter—but I cannot think of many viable reasons to not hire a local attorney.

Of course, with the modern conveniences of telephones, faxes, e-mails, and other Internet communication, it is easy to be in contact with just about anyone, regardless of where that person is. And it is less important to have an attorney who is close to you, physically, than to have one who is experienced in tractor-trailer collisions and a specialist in these types of wrecks, specifically as they pertain to Arkansas law.

You will also probably want to hire someone close to the collision site so that person can go out and take a look around and do some investigating. Your attorney should be familiar with the scene of the collision, and that might be difficult to do if he or she is a few states away or even one state away. Attorneys should be able to easily talk to witnesses or have their staff talk to witnesses. Your attorney should know the local experts and have a solid working relationship with them—a history with them. Your attorney should know which experts do best in front of juries and which ones are not so great when it comes down to courtroom performance.

It is a guarantee that your opposition will hire a very good defense attorney, and it would help your case if your own attorney were somewhat familiar with the opposing attorney, or at least knew something about that attorney's firm. You should find all of these qualities in a local attorney. It is always best to work with an attorney who will know the fine points of your case, from the scene of the collision to all of the players involved.

CHAPTER SEVEN

TRUCKS ARE BIG, BUT NO COLLISION IS TOO SMALL ... OR TOO SLOW

M ost truck accidents involve higher speeds and more significant property damage than other motor collisions, but even slower speeds can cause great bodily injury, due to the weight of trucks.

Insurance adjustors are sometimes skeptical of injury claims in slower-speed collisions because for years, people have exaggerated their injuries for personal gain. I am here to tell you that even the tiniest bump from a tractor-trailer can seriously injure another motorist. There are dozens of variables that can impact how significant an injury is, and speed is only one of them.

Other variables include a collision victim's age, prior health condition, body position at the time of the impact, whether or not the victim knew the collision was about to happen, the headrest position, seat belt use, airbags, steering wheel, and several others. The direction of the impact—from behind, head-on, or from the side—can affect the severity of injuries.

Even at low speeds, a significant amount of tractor-trailer mass hits the other vehicle and therefore causes a more significant amount of injury than would a collision with a smaller vehicle. Even at lower speeds, the amount of energy being transferred from the trailer-truck to a smaller vehicle—a combination of speed plus mass—is significantly more than that transferred from one small vehicle to another small vehicle. Your body will absorb that energy, which may very well cause a more serious injury.

I handled one case I think illustrates this principle really well. It involved a gentleman who was injured in a truck stop parking lot when he was hit by a tractor-trailer. He was a truck driver himself and had just parked his truck when the collision occurred. He had unbuckled his seat belt and was moving from the driver's seat back into the cabin of the tractor, where his bed was. All of a sudden, bang! He felt a jolt. He had been struck by another tractor-trailer moving at less than 10 miles per hour. The other driver had been looking for a parking spot but was not watching where he was going and, as a consequence, bumped my client's truck. It was a little bump, but it had a ripple effect that ended up causing significant damage.

When the collision occurred, my client fell because he was not buckled in. As I mentioned, he had been making his way into the cabin behind the driver's seat to get some rest. He fell backward onto the floor and wrenched his back pretty considerably. He had suffered back problems prior to that collision and had had surgery to try and correct them. And here is an important point to note in any case: a common misconception is that preexisting injuries make a case less valuable. It is just not true.

Insurance adjusters will try to minimize the value of a case, arguing that the prior injury devalues the current injury. They may say that they are responsible only for a portion of the injury because the injury was already there in another form. In Arkansas, and in most states in the country, the defendant is required to pay for all treatment of injuries that are a result of the collision or treatment of the exacerbation of a preexisting injury. In fact, most insurance companies use computer software to evaluate claims and give suggested (or in some cases, mandatory) monetary ranges for their adjusters to negotiate from. Many of these programs are designed to recognize that preexisting conditions make cases more valuable, not less valuable, for the following reason: a preexisting condition predisposes you to further injury and makes it more likely that even a slow-speed impact could cause more bodily damage.

Prior disk damage, prior back damage, and so on make your body a little bit more fragile and therefore more easily damaged in a low-impact collision. The average person might not be badly injured in a slow-speed collision, but someone with a preexisting medical condition could be injured severely. Experienced insurance adjusters in Arkansas recognize this reality, although sometimes they need to be convinced.

My client went to the doctor immediately after his fall in the parking lot collision and underwent an MRI. That test, compared to an MRI done a year earlier, showed a fairly significant change in my client's back, specifically in the disk that had been previously injured. My client now had some disk herniation that had not been present two years before. His case incurred all of the expected prejudices—

including the built-in prejudices that the insurance companies have against low-speed impacts and prior injuries—so he was not able to get the insurance company to make him a settlement offer.

In fact, before he approached me, he had been to a couple of attorneys who had not been able to help him. Finally, one of those attorneys sent him to me. By this time, he had spent more than a year and a half trying to get his case resolved. He had no luck getting any kind of significant offer from the insurance companies, and he could not find an attorney who would be willing to take his case to trial.

When we took on the case, one of the first things we did was order all of the medical records. We ordered not just the medical records from after the wreck but the ones from before the wreck too. That is when we discovered that an MRI had been done a year before the wreck and that we could compare it to the MRI done shortly after the wreck and use that information to our advantage. The two tests made clear the additional damage that had been done to our client as a result of the collision. His doctor, of course, could testify quite clearly about his condition beforehand and his condition afterward.

Because our client had the preexisting condition, he was more susceptible to further injury to his back. He went from having a sore back to having herniated disks that rubbed against nerves, causing him considerable pain, all because of the collision. His doctors recommended surgery as the only appropriate treatment, which he eventually underwent. Although the surgery was successful, it created permanent impairment to his body, as he ended up having to have some of the joints in his lower back fused together.

So it was obvious, in this case, that the speed of the tractor-trailer was not the most significant factor. What was significant was his prior injury and the fact that he was not secured in his seat by his seat belt.

His body was positioned in a way that left him more exposed and vulnerable when he was hit. The weight of the tractor-trailer that hit his vehicle was also a factor, and once again, this is why tractor-trailer cases are different from all other motor vehicle collisions.

We still had to file for litigation because the insurance company would not look past its assumption that my client was exaggerating his injuries. The company never offered him a reasonable amount of compensation, and we were forced to file suit. Once we got into litigation, the insurance company had a chance to review our statements, review his medical records, depose him, and depose the doctors. After we deposed the experts we needed and began looking into the history of the other truck driver, the case ended up settling for $157,000 before it went to trial.

My client had not been offered even a tenth of that before he hired us, and we moved the case into litigation. Sometimes, we have to take such steps to overcome the biases that the insurance companies have toward cases without a significant amount of property damage or cases that do not involve high speeds.

It is important to remember that the insurance adjuster's boss is the insurance company. The bottom line is its profit margin, and insurance adjusters have a responsibility to reduce the value of each claim and not pay a penny more than is necessary. They are more apt to disbelieve a claim of injury or be more skeptical if the claim is not backed up with medical records or sufficient evidence. In fact, even with all of that right in front of them, insurance companies sometimes still do not give the benefit of the doubt to the injured party. Almost universally, if the insurance company doubts a case will resolve in its favor or at least more in its favor, the company will refrain from giving the injured party even the slightest benefit of the doubt. The insurance company will always err on the side of skepticism and on the side that best suits its interest: its bottom line.

Just always remember that no collision is too small or too slow, and if you were injured before the collision or have some other pre-existing condition, it does not count against you in a traffic collision. No one asks to be hit by a tractor-trailer, regardless of how fast or slow it is going, and no one with a preexisting condition wants to do anything to make that condition worse. If you are injured in a collision, you have recourses, no matter how small the collision is.

CHAPTER EIGHT

WHAT MY CASE IS WORTH

There is no exact formula for what your case is worth in Arkansas and, frankly, in most states in the country. That is very different from, say, worker's compensation. If you have ever been involved in a worker's compensation case, you are probably familiar with a formula based on the injury and how long you have suffered. That formula helps you and the other parties involved arrive at the specific amount you may be entitled to. It is sort of a universal formula.

But in a car wreck, specifically in a tractor-trailer case, there is no exact formula for evaluating the value of damages, injury, or loss. There are certain things you are entitled to and certain damages you are entitled to get back from the trucking company. They include your medical expenses—your past and future medical expenses—any scarring, and any past or future wages lost due to incapacity. They also include any pain you suffered for the extent of the injury, care-taking expenses, and other expenses you incurred because of your injury. But the dollar amount of those guaranteed awards varies.

I tell people that the most important factor in determining the value of their case is whether or not the adjuster will pay them what they think they can get away with paying. This, unfortunately, is always—without exception—the lowest amount possible. The only real leverage you have in your case is the jury. So when it comes down to it, your case is worth what a jury would give you for it. Put another way, your case is worth what you (and I) can convince a jury to give us for it.

That is the main thing to remember. You have to treat your case as if it were guaranteed to be going to a jury, because that is the only way we can get full value out of the case. That does not mean we are guaranteed to go before a jury or even guaranteed to go to trial. It just means that if we are prepared to go to trial, we will put the best possible case together. The adjuster will pay an amount based on what he thinks a jury might award and not a penny more. If the possibility of going before a jury does not exist, the adjuster will offer considerably less.

In this chapter, we are going to talk about all of the different factors that juries take into consideration in determining the value of a case, because frankly, the jury is the most authoritative source. There are some values that the adjusters place on cases, and they are usually different from jury amounts. But again, adjustors always aim low. The most important amount and the most accurate amount is what a jury might give. That is the first thing to keep in mind when determining what a case might be worth. Everything we do is based on preparing a case to go to a jury, and putting together the best case possible is paramount. Nothing is more important.

The first thing you are entitled to is an amount for the medical bills you incur. In Arkansas you are entitled to the total amount of the medical bills that are reasonably related to the injury. So the goal is simply determining whether or not the medical bills are related to injuries caused in the wreck or are unrelated to the wreck.

There are a couple of important factors to consider in reaching that evaluation, including how soon after the wreck you began taking medical treatment and if there is consistency from the first treatment through the ongoing treatment. This goes back to the concept we explored earlier: the gap in treatment. You never want to have a gap in your treatment. Nothing good comes out of that, neither for your own health or the success of your case.

One misconception, however, is the more medical expenses you incur, the more valuable your case becomes. That misconception can be a trap, and increasing your medical expenses without a valid medical reason is an easy way to create the opposite effect—one that would actually make your case significantly less valuable.

Of course, you should always get the medical care you need—all of the medical care that is reasonable—but you do not want to over-treat yourself. Do not undertreat and do not overtreat your injury. You simply want to follow the doctor's advice and make sure you are doing everything he tells you to do to help you recover from the injury as quickly as possible.

If your doctor says you need physical therapy to help you recover more quickly, take that advice, because the therapy will probably speed up the healing process and show the jury that you are compliant with the doctor's orders and suggestions. It is not about medical costs. It is about getting the proper care on the proper schedule. That is the best practice for you, and it shows insurance companies and juries that you are earnestly doing your part to make things better.

At times, you may be concerned that you will not be reimbursed for the medical expenses you incur. It is a reasonable concern, but you should never let it influence your decision to receive care. Make sure you get the adequate care you need. You should simply focus on how you can make your body feel and work better and not on your medical bills' impact on the value of your case. Coordinating your benefits and using insurance to pay as many of those bills as possible is important to ensure you don't feel the pressure to under-treat your ailments because you are concerned about the high cost of ever-increasing medical bills.

The amount you receive for pain and suffering and for the extent of your injury is, again, not set in stone. There is no formula for how much each particular type of injury is worth or how much the pain is worth, but juries have to think about these things and consider them when they are determining your award. They should consider what the extent of the pain is, how severe it is, and how long it lasted. This is why, as we discussed in previous chapters, it is so important to keep a journal of all or your activities with an eye toward where it hurts, how it hurts, how long it hurts, and which daily activities you can and cannot do.

The duration and degree of your pain is significant but probably more significant is how that pain affects your daily activities. If it prevents you from doing some things, if it shortens the amount of time you can spend doing certain activities, or if it lengthens the amount of time it normally takes you to do those activities, the jury, and even the insurance company, will consider that when it is time to determine a dollar amount. So the extent of your pain is a factor, but the bigger factor is how that pain affects your daily living.

There are certain things that we know juries react to more strongly than others. One of those things is when an injury prevents you from doing your job. Everyone can relate to that, especially people who sit on a jury and are thus prevented from doing *their* jobs. Jury members are usually sympathetic to anyone who has been forced to miss work due to an injury, and typically, they reimburse those people for any lost wages.

Juries can relate to, and care about, injuries that limit or prevent mobility. We all cherish our mobility because it not only enables us to do the things we want to do but is, from a very basic point of view, our defense mechanism and our survival mechanism. It keeps us alive and allows us to avoid danger. It is a very basic human function that when taken away, causes huge life changes. Anyone can relate to that, and juries always side with the person whose mobility has been taken away. When you have restricted mobility, you are more susceptible to injury, and you are more dependent on others—and people are, by nature, independent beings. We each live in our own body, and our quality of life is directly related to our health. That is probably one of the most significant factors in evaluating what your case may be worth.

Juries react strongly to the fact that your injuries prevent you from doing things around the house that you could do before your collision. Common activities include mowing the lawn or doing the dishes, and you probably want to do as many of those jobs as you can despite the pain. You can continue to push yourself to try and do your housework, the dishes, your lawn mowing, the cleaning, and the laundry. Juries do not punish people for trying harder to accomplish the things they need to accomplish. In fact, they might even be more sympathetic to you if you continue to do those things despite the physical pain they cause you. People know what it is like to have to do something that causes discomfort or even all-out pain, and when jury members relate to the plaintiff, they usually respond appropriately.

Make thorough notes in a journal. If you can still mow the lawn but it takes twice as long as it did before your wreck, write it down, because that is something the folks on the jury can understand. You will show you are trying hard to get over your injury and are not trying to embellish the injury or milk it in any way. If the job takes you longer, or if you cannot finish it, write that down. Being able to do only part of a job is nothing to be ashamed of and certainly nothing to hide. Get that fact out into the open.

Try to do all that you can, and make a note of the things you cannot do and cannot do as fast as you could before the collision. If you have to hire someone to come in and clean your house because you are bedridden and physically unable to get up and do the work, you are entitled to compensation for that. It is not your fault that you have to hire someone. You did not ask for a tractor-trailer to hit you. If it had not hit you, you would be doing your housework yourself. The state of Arkansas understands this and provides the guarantee to you that the party at fault will pay for those services.

The reality these days is that the term *pain and suffering* is not a term attorneys like to use very often. It is outdated, antiquated, and carries a stigma. When we conduct focus groups and talk to juries about case values, we find, pretty consistently, that *pain and suffering* is a term they associate with scam artists—people who try to milk their injuries and get something for nothing. Pain and suffering: what does it mean? It has lost its meaning because it has been overused and abused. Of course, pain is involved, and yes, suffering is too. But when those words are used together in that phrase, they raise a red flag. Juries care more about how the pain affects your daily life and your mobility than the fact that it exists. Of course it exists; that is the whole point of the case.

When we are talking about the value of your case, you must remember that there are some factors that are within your control and some factors that are not within your control. It is obviously important to make sure you are doing everything you should do with regard to factors that are within your control to make sure you do not reduce your case value. These things include following the doctor's orders exactly, not missing appointments, taking the doctor's advice on any referrals or specialists, and taking part in home exercises or physical therapy.

There are a lot of factors that are outside your control and, of course, you do not want to stress those too much. But you have to know what they are so that you know what your case might be worth. Being aware of them will help you determine how to proceed to receive the best settlement possible. In the next section, we will talk a bit about some of those factors you simply cannot control.

We talked earlier about how an injury could affect you, particularly your mobility, and how very important this factor is in determining the value of your claim. In my opinion, the next most important factors are the actions that you and the defendant take and how those actions will look in front of a jury. You, of course, can control how you look, and that is what we talked about with regard to your actions. You want to show that you are doing everything you can to get better, that you are compliant with your doctor's recommendation, that you are following the treatment plan, that you did not do anything to cause the collision, and that you are doing everything you can to get over it.

What we also need to know is how the defendant is going to appear in front of the jury. This is one of the things we cannot control. Juries react to individuals, and they will award more or less depending on how they view you and how they view the defendant. To that end, you need to find out as much as you can about the defendant so you know how that person will present himself or herself and come across in front of a jury. That may involve knowing if he or she has a criminal record or a bad driving record. It may include whether or not the defendant is taking full responsibility for the collision. If the defendant caused the wreck but is not willing to be accountable for the things that contributed to the collision, juries will react negatively. They expect all parties involved to be accountable for the things they have done and the harms they have caused. Any lack of accountability will affect how the jury determines the judgment amount, which directly affects the plaintiff.

The defendant's refusal to take responsibility is something we can determine right from the start, based on statements made in the police report. You will want to see if the defendant took full responsibility for the collision or tried to push the responsibility off on you or somebody else. If pushing the responsibility onto someone else is unreasonable, it will only help our case more. The same goes for insurance adjusters. They won't want to tip you off to their position, but you can, sometimes, pick up clues as to whether they are disputing their liability or owning up to their responsibility.

You might have discussions with them, but again, I recommend that you tell them as little as possible until you decide whether to hire an attorney or not because almost everything you say to the adjuster is going to be recorded, kept, and used against you in any way possible. If you have discussions with an insurance adjuster, you may get some clues on how he or she will present the case in front of a jury and whether or not the adjuster's company will take full responsibility or try to shirk its responsibility. This can help us in creating our own strategy in front of a jury or in the case in general. So while some things are out of our control, we can take clues from them to gain control in other areas.

As I have mentioned several times before, tractor-trailer cases are different from all other motor vehicle cases and, with that in mind, you should also know that juries expect tractor-trailer drivers to be held to a higher standard. To reiterate a few of the criteria: the driver should hold a commercial driver's license, which means he went through more extensive training than the average driver. Because of this he should also have a better understanding of the safety rules and regulations of driving and a better understanding of how to drive defensively.

A tractor-trailer, generally, carries a much bigger cargo load—much more dangerous cargo, to put it another way—than a smaller vehicle and therefore takes longer to come to a stop. On top of that, everything the drivers do is in the name of profit, their own and their trucking company's. Because of all of this and some other factors, truck drivers must be held to a higher standard than the average motorist.

The law and procedural rules are designed to make sure that you are made whole after being injured in a motor vehicle collision. The law ensures that you are protected because another important factor to remember is that you are the only one who did not ask to be involved in the litigation process. Everybody else asked to be a part of this process. The trucking company makes a profit from driving its trucks and hauling goods from one place to another, and it will continue to do that because that is integral to its bottom line.

The medical providers make a profit from providing medical care to patients injured in wrecks, and so they asked to be a part of this process. The insurance companies design their profit margins to take account of charging you a premium and paying you when you claim compensation for damage incurred from any wreck you are unfortunate enough to be involved in. That is part of their business model, and so they expect to be involved in this type of situation regularly. Thus, they asked to be a part of the process. Even the attorneys are involved of their own choice because the litigation process is how they earn a living. The same goes for the experts. They get paid to offer their opinions and, if it comes down to it, their testimonies.

So everybody has asked to be part of the legal process except you, and the law recognizes this and does what it can to try to get you made whole and compensated adequately to put you back into the position you were in before the wreck happened. It is important to keep in mind throughout the entire life of the case that you are the only one who did not ask to be involved.

Juries understand that commercial truck drivers do what they do on a regular basis. Juries understand that truck drivers drive five days a week almost every week of the year to make a profit. With all of this in mind, juries expect truck drivers to be safer than everyone else on the road. They expect truck drivers to not take any steps that would needlessly endanger the public, and they expect that the companies employing the drivers would not take any steps to needlessly endanger the public.

So it is important to recognize that when a jury determines that a driver or a trucking company did something that needlessly endangered the public, it affects the value of the case. There is no formula. It is a purely human process. The jury considers the driver's negligence and the trucking company's negligence just as much as it considers your medical expenses. Even when the jury weighs factors that have no obvious dollar amount attached to them (what is "fault" worth?), the jury is able to assign a value to it. That is why it is so difficult to say what a case is worth. The only thing you can say with certainty is a case is worth what a jury says it is worth once that jury considers all of the factors involved. But there are things we can do to influence the jury to give us the biggest settlement possible. Read on to find out more about that.

CHAPTER NINE

THE FINER POINTS OF DETERMINING THE VALUE OF YOUR CASE

In all tractor-trailer cases, there is evidence, and there are facts of law. But do you know what else there is? The process can get personal. What the defendant did and how he responded to what he did are two big factors that the jury looks at. The jury also looks at the "person" that the driver is. Jury members are human beings, and their personal opinions and biases enter into the equation all the time. If they simply do not like the defendant or you, it will affect their verdict and the value of the case. Your demeanor and the demeanor of the defendant are important to the jury, and we are not just talking about courtroom demeanor. It goes all the way back to the scene of the collision. It includes the demeanor you display when you are being treated by your doctor.

If the defendant was belligerent, loud, or verbally abusive to anybody at the time of the wreck, we will make sure that the jury knows that, because that kind of behavior will not work in favor of the defendant. Of course, we love it if the defendant acts that way in front of the jury when we are in the middle of a trial. We want the defendant to be rude or belligerent or arrogant because we know that the jury will take it into consideration. But short of that, we at least try to find instances of rudeness or belligerence somewhere during the process. Juries do not give awards to people they do not like. Knowing this, we make sure you are the picture of pleasantness throughout the entire process, even when things get stressful. We will help you as best we can with that. These cases might seem very procedural and mechanical, but there is a human element involved in all of it, and we can never lose sight of it.

In addition to how you or the defendant acted at the scene of the collision, which probably lasted a relatively short period of time, there are plenty of opportunities to lose focus and let your emotions get the best of you. Remember that a trial is not a 15-minute or 45-minute formal proceeding. It takes days or weeks to get through a jury trial, and that can try the patience of the parties involved. Your emotions are going to come out, and your personality is going to come out. If you are a kind, reasonable person, the jury will more than likely pick up on that. If you are easily riled or get frustrated or arrogant, the jury is going to pick up on that as well. Your behavior will make a big difference one way or another in the value of the case. We will do everything we can to coach you and help you keep your cool.

In Arkansas, and in almost every state, we have what we call the golden rule, which states quite simply that an attorney is not allowed to tell jury members to put themselves in either the plaintiff's or the defendant's position. Neither the defendant's nor the plaintiff's attorney is allowed to tell the jury, "This is what you should do because this is what you would want to have happen if you were in their position." That's called the golden rule, and you cannot make golden-rule arguments in courts.

That said, we know that juries do it anyway because human beings are empathetic. That is the reality of what happens in front of a jury. Juries drive on the highways. They have kids who drive on the highways. They have grandkids who drive or ride on the highways. They want to know that the streets are safe. They want to know that people are driving carefully and defensively and not taking any steps that will endanger the public unnecessarily. So even though we have the golden rule, juries put themselves in the shoes of the two parties all the time. Again, it is the human factor.

If a jury feels that you or the other side would have put them or their children or grandchildren at risk, they will suddenly, and maybe without thinking much about it, make an award based on that perception. They will take some action in an attempt to defend themselves or to protect themselves, even if it is completely subconscious on their part. There is not much you can do to prevent that or to enhance that. But you have to be aware of it and recognize that it can happen in a trial and is one of the things we have to accept. We also have to remember that the jury's perception is likely to affect the value of your case.

Tractor-trailer cases are better for the plaintiffs than other cases, because most of the time, jury members realize how scared they are of big trucks. They do not like being cut off by tractor-trailers changing lanes, and they feel some danger when they see or think about tractor-trailers. Those feelings also contribute to the higher values awarded in tractor-trailer cases.

I handled a case involving two guys whom we will call Mike and Bill. They were hit by a tractor-trailer as they were driving on the interstate. The other tractor-trailer was passing them in the fast lane and suddenly swerved into them, pushing them toward the shoulder. Mike was driving, and he managed to keep the truck on the highway. The first collision was followed by a second one just like the first but harder. This one ran them completely off the shoulder, into the grass, and almost into a concrete culvert. Mike missed smashing into the culvert by only about ten feet. Had they hit the culvert, they probably both would have died, but they escaped the wreck without life-threatening injuries. Still, they each had some significant injuries, including a shoulder separation for Mike and a wrist injury for Bill.

When we were evaluating that case, we looked at all of the factors that we have already explored in this book. We looked at how the shoulder injury affected Mike, how much it affected his ability to do his yard work. He was not able to mow the lawn as much anymore. He could not do as much yard work as he had been able to before the wreck. Some of the activities he liked to do during his off time were difficult for him. He liked to play golf but could not play golf at all for a number of months. His shoulder pain would not allow him to swing a club. We weighed all of those different factors to determine what his case might be worth, and we did the same thing for Bill. We documented how much the wrist injury affected his work and how much it affected the things that he normally liked to do. Hearing those details and that loss of mobility and freedom are what really hit home with the jury. But the issue that had the most significant effect on the value of the case was the action of the defendant.

We learned, first, that the defendant had been under the influence of illegal drugs at the time he caused this wreck, which, of course, immediately increased the value of the case in our minds. Regardless of what the case value had been before we learned that, we knew that simply adding that additional fact would help our cause. The defendant was on methamphetamine, so we knew that when the jury heard the defendant was driving a commercial vehicle under the influence of such a dangerous drug, the value of the case would increase significantly.

We then learned a few more things about the actions of the defendant, and they all continued to increase the value of our case over and above what the value of the injuries alone would have been. One thing we found after looking at the vehicles was that the defendant's tractor-trailer hit our clients once, knocking them onto the shoulder, and then accelerated before striking them the second time and knocking them completely off the road. So after the defendant collided with my clients, he actually accelerated and collided with them again. That was a major factor, as you can imagine.

The way we determined this was through the tractor-trailer's exhaust pipes, which extended above the vehicle and emitted black smoke when the accelerator was pushed down hard. This happened after the first collision, and the smoke stained the side of the tractor-trailer near the place of the second impact. So the defendant was under the influence of methamphetamine, a dangerous and powerful stimulant, and after he hit my clients the first time, he accelerated and hit them again. He probably would not have done that had he not been under the influence of that drug. These significant bits of evidence increased the value of the case significantly.

There was even one more factor in our favor. We learned that there had been two 911 calls about the defendant's driving in the 90 minutes leading up to the collision with my clients, as the defendant made his way across Oklahoma and into Arkansas on the interstate.

Other people had been worried enough about his driving and the danger he posed to the public to call the emergency police line and report him. Once again, it was a factor that increased the value of our case, which we eventually settled in the weeks before the trial was set to begin. All of those issues played a part in the final evaluation, and each one increased the value of the claim for Mike and Bill.

In that case, as in so many others, all factors played a role in determining what the case was worth. It matters if the defendant driver took a defensive driving course prior to the collision and how often the driver took that defensive driving course. It matters if the driver is serious about driver safety, because it tells a jury whether the driver's actions need to be fixed.

Does the trucking company inspect its vehicles? Does the company, before every trip, conduct an inspection of the brakes, of the tires, of the electrical system, of the fire extinguishers, and of all the different components a trucking company is required to monitor? Does the company do everything it can to make sure its vehicles won't endanger anybody? Is the company being as safe as possible? All of those things are considered by a jury, which—I cannot say it often enough—is made up of human beings who drive cars every day just as you and I do.

Juries want to hold faulty drivers and trucking companies responsible, and the only way to do that is through their pocketbooks. We cannot put them in jail for their actions. We do not allow vigilante justice. In the civil court system, we hold people accountable through monetary means, and we believe that if we hold them accountable, they will change their behavior. We trust they will be safer and more responsible drivers. One key to increasing the value of your case is knowing all of the ways in which the defendant driver and trucking company were not being safe.

Distraction and fatigue are big factors too. We want to know if the driver was distracted. Was he talking or texting on a cell phone while he was driving? Was he maintaining his logbook properly and being honest about the amount of rest he was getting versus the number of hours he spent driving? Was he driving for a reasonable number of hours at a stretch, or was he driving too much?

You never know for sure what you are going to find out, as we learned in the case of Mike and Bill. New details just kept coming out, doubling and tripling the amount of our original estimate of the case's value. Many times, one crucial fact can make the difference between a case that has very little value and a case that has a lot of value. In the case of Mike and Bill, it was three new details. One new detail is good, but three is great.

Earlier, I related a story about someone who met a truck head-on, on a rural, dirt road that was barely wide enough for two cars to pass each other. One key piece of evidence was the existence of a "No Thru Trucks" sign that should have deterred the truck driver from being on that road in the first place. In that scenario, even after some of the initial discovery had been done, and even after we brought in an expert to talk about the "No Thru Trucks" sign, the defense might have increased the value by only a couple of hundred thousand dollars. We later discovered that the driver had not done a pre-trip inspection, which meant that he had neglected to check whether the fire extinguishers were in proper working order. We learned that the driver had not kept up with his annual physicals as required. That was another factor that increased the value. The very next offer we got from the insurance company was double the amount of the previous offer. Things can change that fast, and insurance companies always fight to pay out as little as they can get away with. It is our job to unearth the details that will show in how many ways our opponent was being unsafe or negligent.

I had another case involving a man we will call Allen, who was hit by a tractor-trailer. The 18-wheeler driver had taken a curve too quickly, and his truck turned over on its side and skidded down the road, sliding into Allen's vehicle and crushing Allen's leg in the collision. It was obvious that the truck driver was at fault, and the insurance company attempted to settle the claim quickly, assuring the client that they would pay all of his damages. They made an initial offer that many people (and attorneys) would consider a lot of money.

But we saw some red flags in the company's safety record and investigated the cause of the wreck further. We discovered a crack in the hitch of the tractor. It was determined that the crack had some oxidation in it, suggesting that it had been there for some time. The trailer had broken off from the cab of the truck when the truck turned on its side, and it was the sliding trailer that crushed Allen. Once we discovered the crack, it became obvious that the trucking company had not been inspecting its equipment. The cracked trailer hitch was a disaster waiting to happen and could have been easily prevented long before Allen's leg was crushed. As a result of that investigation, the value of the case increased significantly. Once again, the case went from one set of numbers to a much higher set of numbers because of one additional factor that came into play in the process. That cracked hitch contributed to the truck driver's loss of control, the trailer's detachment from the tractor, and its slide down the road into a collision.

I had a case when I first started practicing that involved a kid who was about 13 years old. His parents had gotten a new tractor—a farm tractor. It was a used tractor that they had bought from a certified dealer. Without getting into brand names, let's just say that it was a tractor from a reputable manufacturer. It was used, but the certified dealer had inspected it, and presumably, tested it before selling it to this family with some sort of seal of approval attached to it.

Farm tractors are designed to have a safety mechanism that prevents the operator from starting the engine if the tractor is in gear or if the operator is not sitting in the seat. For obvious reasons, you do not want anyone to start a tractor up if the tractor is in gear or if a qualified driver is not sitting in the seat. That is exactly what happened in this case. The family had had the tractor for a week, and their son, whom we will call Nathanial, started it up while it was already in gear. The force pushed him forward and threw him to the ground, and then the tractor rolled over him and ended up breaking bones in his leg.

We took on the case. Since we were dealing with a used tractor and not a tractor direct from the manufacturer, our first question was whether or not the manufacturer should have known about this problem. We were wondering if this tractor's ability to start when it was in gear was a design flaw. We had an expert look at the tractor, and he discovered that the safety wire that prevented the tractor from being started while it was in gear had been bypassed with a paperclip. A simple paperclip had been slipped into a spot that would allow the necessary ignition to take place even if the tractor was in gear, and that is why the tractor was able to start in gear, roll forward, and roll over our client.

Of course, the other side, the certified dealer, argued that there was no way the dealership could have known that somebody had put a paper clip in there to bypass that mechanism—and it could have even been our client who had done it. But when the expert looked at the paper clip, he determined that it had a significant amount of rust on it. There was also rust on a nearby piece of metal, which had fused itself to the paper clip. From that evidence, we were able to conclude that the paper clip had been in that spot for at least a couple of years, meaning there was no way that our client could have put it there.

If the certified dealer had done a full inspection of the trailer, he would have noticed that the bypass switch had been modified by the previous owner using that paper clip. The dealer had certified the used tractor, and for a long time he denied liability for the malfunction and the boy's broken leg. But, finally, we got the case resolved for a reasonable amount of money.

I have handled a lot of cases involving motor vehicle collisions and tractor-trailer collisions from which witnesses have emerged later in the process and significantly affected the value of the cases or changed our strategy. You want to conduct as thorough an investigation as possible so you can uncover as many of those witnesses as possible early on. You do not want any surprises. You want to know what to expect.

In a disputed liability case I once handled, a witness for the opposition came in late and torpedoed us. It was a red light collision case, and both sides argued that they had had a green light, and therefore, the right of way. We were not able to find any witnesses who could really say with authority one way or the other who had the red and who had the green. We eventually had to file suit because the insurance company refused to pay us and was adamant that its driver had the green light and our driver had the red light.

Well, about five months into litigation, a witness emerged. She had been at her place of employment near the intersection during the collision, and she, as I mentioned, effectively torpedoed our case. She testified that our client had had the red light and that our client went through the red light. She was a credible witness, and there was not much we could do. It seemed very clear that she had been where she said she had been and that she had seen the collision. The case was over.

Her testimony had a significant negative value on the case from our point of view. What we had earlier deemed to be a good case with a lot of damages (because our client had suffered some broken bones in the wreck) became a case that was really worth zero to us because we did not know of all the facts. When that last bit of information came out from the surprise witness, it was clear that the other driver had had the right of way and our client had not. We got torpedoed, and we were sunk. Most times, things like this work in our favor because we work hard to find them.

One fine point here is that when you are working with an attorney, you should always make sure that the attorney knows everything that you know. Never withhold information from your attorney. The more you tell your attorney, the better. Let your attorney sift through your information and decide which of it is relevant or important and which of it can be discarded. It is much better to have more information than you can use than to not have enough because some of it exists only in your head. Communicate and share everything you know about your case with your attorney. It is your attorney's job to properly represent you and present all of the facts, all of the evidence, that help your case. If there are things your attorney does not know about you, or your case, he or she cannot prepare well on your behalf. That can be devastating to your case later, especially if the information you are withholding somehow comes to benefit your opponent when it could have benefited you.

You have to assume, with all of the resources the trucking industry has, that your opponent is going to know a lot more about you, on average, than your own attorney does. Your opponent is going to search your social media sites, such as Facebook and Twitter accounts. Everything that you do online, your opponent is going to know about. Your opponent will also know your insurance history. Give all of that information, and much more, to your attorney. It will only help your case.

In fact, there is an Insurance Services Office (ISO) database that allows insurance companies to keep track of all of your claims—literally, any insurance claims you have made and what they were for. Your attorney may have access to that information as well but for a fee. The insurance company always has access to that. It will know how many wrecks you have been in before, if you have claimed a neck injury, or if you have had back injuries. The only way your attorney will know this is if you tell him or her. And how easy is that? It is important to let your attorney know all of these things so he or she can properly advise you and properly evaluate your case. Otherwise, you will be giving all of the arrows to the defense, and you will be stuck holding an empty quiver. You will not help your attorney to come up with a realistic assessment of the value of your case.

If you have had three or four previous claims for similar injuries, let your attorney know. Remember that huge misconception: that preexisting injuries hurt the value of your case. It is not true. Preexisting injuries do not hurt your case, ever. I have had many cases that have gone south fast primarily because my clients in those cases failed to tell me about their preexisting injuries for fear that they would decrease the value of our current case. In fact, they can often help increase the value of the current case. It depends on how the wreck affected that injury.

Having a preexisting condition makes you more likely to get hurt again from a wreck. It often makes the injury more serious because you had already had problems with your back or your neck, and now, because of your most recent collision, it has gotten to the point where you are unable to even walk. You might now have to have surgery, whereas you did not have to have surgery before, even though your back or neck was injured. That is not a negative for you in terms of your case. That is a positive.

A client's preexisting injury is never something that we shy away from. We usually like to draw attention to it. We have to tackle those situations head-on and find out the extent of the preexisting injury, and when it works in our favor, we put it out there, front and center. We need to know everything about you, including all of the doctors you saw beforehand, and if that information appears to work in our favor, we use it.

Many times, it is actually easier to prove a case with a preexisting injury because if you received a fair amount of treatment for that earlier injury, you probably have a whole file of X-rays that show exactly what your injury looked like before the wreck. We can show those older X-rays side-by-side with the new X-rays to prove how much the most recent collision has worsened your injury. It is usually very clear and almost always works in our favor. Cases often become more valuable once we introduce a preexisting condition. Not only can we talk about how the wreck has made the preexisting injury worse, but we can also speculate as to how the current injury might degenerate in the future. If you have a preexisting injury of any kind, tell your attorney about it. It will probably help your case in the long run.

But the first rule to remember is that it does not matter if a preexisting injury makes your case less valuable or more valuable. We need to know about that previous injury because we need to know about everything. Period. Hiding things is usually a path to destruction and zero verdicts. If a jury believes that you are hiding information or lying about something, it can affect your case significantly. They need to like you and believe you and trust you. There is nothing a jury hates more than being lied to or feeling that they are being deceived. So it is just a good idea to be forthcoming and honest about everything, and it all starts with your attorney. When an insurance adjustor calls you, give him as little information as possible. But when your attorney asks you for information, any information at all, spill your guts.

One specific area of injury that we are beginning to understand better is traumatic brain injuries. We now know that when you experience a concussion and then experience additional ones, the later concussions become a lot more severe because of the earlier one. So if you had concussions in your past, and you suffer a traumatic brain injury in a collision later, it is likely going to have a more devastating effect on you than it would on someone who had never had a concussion before.

The same principle applies to all of this. Often, conditions you experienced earlier in life make your latest injuries more severe, and the only way to know if this is the case is to fully evaluate your medical records. Your attorney should know about all of the doctors you have seen so he or she can compare your prior medical records with your current ones.

I could go on about traumatic brain injuries for hours, but generally, if you lost consciousness at all in a collision, you need to talk to your doctor about traumatic brain injuries. You need to make sure that you have been thoroughly checked out and properly diagnosed. If you have a traumatic brain injury, you cannot afford to let it go undiagnosed. This type of injury is serious and can have long-lasting effects. You need to have a discussion with your doctor about traumatic brain injuries early on. You also need to make sure that your family is clear about the symptoms of a traumatic brain injury so that they can help determine if you are experiencing any cognitive changes after your wreck. Your head does not need to be hit very hard to suffer a traumatic brain injury. You might not even feel severe pain. If you feel you have hit your head or had your head jolted in any way during a wreck, get it checked out in every way possible. Always err on the side of caution and get as thorough a medical examination as possible.

The focus of this book has been on motor vehicle collisions with tractor-trailers, but you may have been in a collision with another motor vehicle, a bicycle, a motorcycle, or a pedestrian. So it is also important to know how to value those cases and how to apply relevant factors in the evaluations. Read on to find out more about these other types of collisions.

CHAPTER TEN

OTHER TYPES OF COLLISIONS

M y primary focus, of course, is tractor-trailer collisions. But through the years I have represented clients in all kinds of automobile collisions. Even though much of my experience is with tractor-trailer wrecks, I still handle other types of traffic collisions. There are important factors common to all wrecks, but others are specific to the vehicles or pedestrians involved in the wreck.

CAR VERSUS CAR

If you were hit by another small motor vehicle, many of the factors discussed up to this point in this book are not going to play a role in your case. You are obviously not going to be looking for the other driver's logbooks, for proof that he or she has been through defensive driving classes, or for any kind of information about the company that employs him or her. But you will still want to know if the other driver was fatigued, had been driving longer than was safe to do so, or had been trying to drive on an all-night trip without a break from

Florida to Oklahoma and then going through Arkansas during the fifteenth or eighteenth hour of that trip.

You will want to know if the other driver was talking on a cell phone or texting someone. You will want to know the other driver's driving history, too, because all of these things affect the value of your case, in addition to the factors you control. To say it another way, the factors you control probably will be the same in most cases. Your injuries, the extent of your injuries, and your preexisting conditions are universally relevant regardless of the kind of collision you were in.

But it is the actions of the defendant that may change significantly. With car cases, the distraction issues are sometimes the most important. Cars have electronic data just as tractor-trailers do, so it still may be necessary to obtain a copy of that data from the vehicle that hit you. This would be particularly crucial if the collision occurred in a high-speed area or wherever speed may have been a factor in the collision. Maintenance records are also important in vehicle collisions. I have had hydroplane cases that have hinged on whether or not the defendant knew that his tires were bald and should have replaced them. You need to know if those factors were present and whether or not they will play a role in your case.

I have been involved in cases in which the defendant rear-ended my clients and then said, "Hey, I tried to stop, but my brakes went out," or "My brakes failed." What they are really trying to say is, "I'm not responsible. It is not my fault that my brakes failed. It was my car's fault or the mechanic's fault." And maybe it was. But we have to look into that. We have to see when that person last had his brakes checked and by whom. Was it a certified, reputable auto mechanic, or was it his 16-year-old nephew who was halfway through his first high-school auto shop class? How often did the defendant get the brakes checked, and when was the most recent time? Three weeks ago? Three years ago? Was the defendant taking reasonable steps to maintain the proper working condition of his brakes? All of these things are factors in motor vehicle cases.

CAR VERSUS MOTORCYCLE

In motorcycle cases, again, many of the same rules apply, but if you were on a motorcycle, the defendant will often claim that he or she could not see you. This could apply to a motorcycle or a bicycle, and again, it is the defendant saying, "It's not my fault I hit you, because I could not see you." Certainly, it is the responsibility of every driver to see everything that is out in front of him, so that excuse is not usually going to hold up. All motorists are responsible for seeing motorcyclists and bicyclists, reacting to them safely, and not making moves that would endanger them. Often, injuries are more severe in motorcycle or bicycle collisions simply because the riders are not protected against the much larger, much heavier car.

With regard to motorcycle, bicycle, and car wrecks, a couple of things are not factors in Arkansas. One is seat belts. Whether or not you were wearing a seat belt is not something that is admissible evidence in Arkansas courtrooms. Insurance companies cannot rely on that factor, and juries cannot consider it, one way or the other, when determining what the value of your case might be. It is always a good idea to wear a seat belt when you are driving—for your own safety—but it will have nothing to do with the value of your case in the end. Helmet laws change too. Just because something is good for you personally does not mean it is good (or bad) for your case.

CAR VERSUS PEDESTRIAN

A common misconception is that if you were a pedestrian struck by a motor vehicle and you were not in a crosswalk at the time of the collision, you would not have a case. Again, this is just not true. Drivers are required to look out for everything in their path, including other cars, trucks, motorcycles, bicycles, and pedestrians. Certainly, if you were to jump out into the street or dart out from behind a parked car and into the path of an oncoming car, you would probably not be able to argue that the motorist should have avoided hitting you. Drivers are human, and their reflexes and reaction times do have limits.

But if you are walking across a road, on a crosswalk or not, and a driver does not slow down or is not paying attention and strikes you, the driver is responsible for that collision. The bottom line is drivers are responsible for keeping an eye out for pedestrians and avoiding them when they enter the roadway, whether they are in a designated crosswalk or not. Even if pedestrians were to cross a street in the middle of the block, where motorists would least expect them, motorists should be aware of the pedestrians, slow down, and let them cross unharmed. This is one unique thing about pedestrians: they can kind of come and go as they please, and they are almost always protected.

CHAPTER ELEVEN

IMPORTANT DO'S AND DON'TS FOR YOUR TRACTOR-TRAILER COLLISION

There are a lot of specific words and phrases that come up over the course of a tractor-trailer collision case, and you might not be familiar with them at first. There are also ways to talk to adjusters and juries, and your attorney is well versed in all of this. He can help you communicate as best you can and understand some things that, normally, would not make sense to you.

Your understanding and the way you communicate can make a big difference in how you handle your case and whether or not you get a good resolution to it. Talking to an insurance adjuster, or to a jury, can be a crucial part of your case. It is important that you go into those situations armed with all of the information you need to get the most out of that interaction and thus help increase the odds of your case being more valuable than it would otherwise have been.

The way you talk to an insurance adjuster is important, but nothing is more important than how you talk to a jury. Remember that when we take on a case and begin putting it together, we do everything on the assumption that we will go to a jury trial. If we do that, even if we do not end up in a trial, we will have done everything correctly and will have maximized the value of the case. Actually, we will also increase the odds that we will not go before a jury. Yes, you read that right. By assuming that we are going to go to trial and preparing as if we are going to trial, we will likely avoid going to trial. If we have a solid, thorough case, our opposition will not want to go to trial because they know they will lose.

DON'T GIVE TOO MUCH AWAY

We start building our strong case immediately. So when the insurance adjuster calls, it is important for you to know how to speak to that person. You have to keep in mind that the adjuster is listening for even the slightest, most subtle little thing you say that can be later used against you or at least in favor of the insurance company. Adjusters try to get plaintiffs to say things that they can later use if the case goes before a jury. One of the things they try to get plaintiffs to say, just a few days after the wreck, is that they are feeling fine. Adjusters will not ask for the specifics of the injury, just how the plaintiff is doing generally. If the plaintiff says, "I'm doing okay," or "I'm doing fine. How are you?" the adjuster will absolutely use that against the plaintiff later in the case.

Adjusters look for power words that make it sound as if the injuries are not very bad. They want to be able to use those words down the road to show that the plaintiff cannot have had a traumatic brain injury that is causing long-term problems because the plaintiff said he or she was fine. An adjuster wants to claim the plaintiff cannot have a knee problem that is going to require surgery or a back problem that is going to require surgery because the plaintiff told the adjuster five days after the wreck that he or she was okay.

The insurance adjuster, quite simply, will try to trick you, deceive you, and coerce you into saying things that will help the insurance company's side of the case. Be wary of this because the adjuster is likely recording everything. When the adjuster calls you for that initial statement, he or she will try to make you feel more positive about the wreck and look for words that will help minimize the value of your claim.

This does not mean that you need to exaggerate your injuries when you talk to an adjuster. It just means that you should not volunteer anything that can be used against you. If you can avoid talking to the adjuster altogether, that's even better. Frankly, it is almost never in your best interest to speak with an insurance adjuster about your injuries until you are done treating them and you know the full extent of them. Only then, when you understand what the consequences of those injuries are going to be from that point forward, should you consider talking to an adjuster. Talking about your injuries before all of the information is in is just a recipe for disaster. That is the first rule.

The second rule is if you still choose to talk to an insurance adjuster because you may think you want to settle on your own (without the aid of an attorney) or because you are not sure what you want to do and you want to hear what the adjuster has to offer, just make sure that you avoid giving too many descriptive or conclusive statements about how you are feeling. Explain what your specific symptoms are. You do not need to say what your symptoms are not. That does not matter because there are a million things that your symptoms are not. Just say what your symptoms are in the simplest, most direct way possible.

Do not say you are not feeling any pain in your hand, even if your hand is close to your injury. Where you are not having pain, no matter where it is on your body, has nothing to do with your injury. You could go down the list of all of the places you are not feeling pain. Are you feeling any pain in your right toe? Or your left toe? Or your eyebrow? Or your finger? There are probably a thousand places you are not feeling pain. The only place that matters is the place where you are feeling pain or experiencing some kind of symptom. Maybe you are not feeling pain, but you cannot move a certain part of your body. Tell the adjuster. Do not talk about all—or any—body parts you are able to move just fine. Only describe areas that are in pain or somehow different now than they were before the wreck.

Be as brief and direct as possible, and let the adjuster know if you are seeing a doctor or not. Sometimes the best thing to do is simply say you will forward the information later. You do not need to get into specifics on that first call. Visit your doctor, get some information from him, and then relay it to the insurance adjuster. Make the adjuster adhere to your schedule, not the other way around.

Again, do not give the adjuster one bit of information more than is necessary. There is no need to describe your symptoms in detail because if there is some detail you leave out, it could come back to haunt you later. The adjuster will make sure to point that out in front of a jury. If you have six symptoms, and you name only four or five because you are tired or just not feeling one of them at that moment because of the painkillers that have been prescribed for you, the adjuster will bring that up later, saying you had your chance to list your symptoms and you never said anything about the pain in your elbow that you are now describing to the jury. This can hurt your case in many ways.

DON'T GUESS

If you come off as being unreliable, it can be devastating to your case. Leaving out information is one thing, but saying something that could be construed as a lie is much worse. The other important thing that we tell clients before they take depositions is that they should never guess. The same rule applies if you talk to an adjuster before you hire an attorney. Do not guess. Tell the adjuster what your symptoms are, but do not guess anything. The primary reason for this is if you guess and you guess wrong, it could be construed as a lie when the adjuster's recording is played for the jury or when an opposing attorney asks you the same question in front of a jury and gets a different answer than the one you gave months earlier to the adjuster.

This happens frequently with older clients. Even if I have talked to them and prepared them and gone over our questions and answers several times, sometimes, older people will give a different answer from the one they gave weeks earlier. Say there is a 65-year-old man sitting in front of a deposition, and he has a back problem that was caused by a wreck, and he needs to have surgery. The attorney says, "Did you have any back problems before the wreck?" Well, he is 65 years old. Will he remember every time in his life when he mentioned a back problem to a doctor? The odds are that he will not. In fact, I do not think any human being would remember. So the first impulse of anyone who has not had significant back problems before the wreck is to say no. When the question is asked, "Did you have any back problems prior to this wreck?" the claimant's impulse is to say, "No, I didn't." That is the likely answer a claimant will give if not prepared.

Well, guess what? If, at age 40, you had seen a doctor because you had high blood pressure or because you had the flu, and you also pointed out to the doctor that your back was sore—that it had been hurting for a couple days because you slept on it wrong or you wrenched it picking something up—the doctor is going to write in your report, "Lower back pain." He will treat it in some way and make recommendations to you on how to treat it at home.

The defense is going to have that medical report, guaranteed. And so, at this juncture, they will say, "Wait a second. You told us that you never had any back problems before. It says here that you saw your doctor for a back problem in 1995. How come you did not tell us about that when we asked you?" That is an example of a guess that can be turned into what appears to be a lie, even if it is not. Do not guess, ever. Do not guess in a conversation with an insurance adjuster or in a deposition. Of course, never lie either. Most of our clients already know not to lie; they know how devastating that can be. But the thing that can trip you up is guessing, because if you guess and you guess wrong, it will look like a lie.

DON'T SAY "ACCIDENT", BUT DO SAY "COLLISION" OR "WRECK"

We have words we want to be sure to use and others that we do not when it comes to characterizing the events of your case. One word we never want to use is accident. We want to say either "collision" or "wreck." The adjuster and the defense attorney will most frequently refer to your motor vehicle collision as an "accident." What that is subtly implying is that it was nobody's fault. Accidents happen, and we know that accidents happen.

Sometimes accidents happen and nobody is at fault. But in traffic collisions, very rarely is no one at fault. Very rarely could a collision not have been prevented. Ninety-nine percent of motor vehicle collisions are due to driver error. So virtually all of our car collisions could have been prevented if everybody had followed the rules and done what they were supposed to do. When a tractor-trailer smashed into your car, you were involved in a collision or a wreck—not an accident.

It was not an accident unless a meteorite fell from the sky, landed three feet in front of your car, and you struck it. That would be an unfortunate accident. An accident happens when a deer jumps out from the woods and into the side of your car, and you have no time to react. A tractor-trailer colliding with another vehicle because the driver was exceeding the speed limit, driving longer than he was supposed to, following too closely behind the other vehicle, or not keeping a proper lookout is not an accident. It is a preventable wreck. It may be a subtle difference of vocabulary, but it is an important difference nonetheless. Never say "accident." Say "collision" or "wreck" every time. It will make a difference in front of a jury if it comes down to that. Even if your case never makes it to trial, saying "collision" or "wreck" is just a good habit to get into from the very start of the case.

DON'T CALL IT WHIPLASH

The reality is that when you are in a rear-end collision or are hit from behind by a tractor-trailer or any other motor vehicle, the most likely place you will be injured is your neck. In the past, this injury has usually been referred to as a "whiplash." It is a common injury, and the reason it occurs is obvious. Think of your head as a bowling ball attached to your body by a thousand fishing lines, and then think about your spine connecting those fishing lines to the rest of your body.

When you are hit from behind, your body gets pushed forward. The fact is that when the seat reacts to the force from that impact, it pushes your back, torso, and legs forward, but your head will not follow at the same rate of speed. Usually, your head will whip back before it catches up with the rest of your body. So again, imagine a ten-pound bowling ball attached to a 150-pound torso by a bunch of wires or fishing lines. When the torso is pushed forward, the bowling ball stays where it is until the lines catch it and snap it back into place. If your headrest is at the proper height to prevent your head from whipping back, it will at least push your head forward at the same speed the seat pushes your body forward, and you are less likely sustain a whiplash injury, and any injury is likely to be less severe.

So an injury may be avoided if your headrest is in the perfect position and your head is up against it. But when you are riding in a car, your head is usually not leaning against the headrest, which means that if you get into a collision, your head is probably not leaning against the headrest either. Most of us sit upright with our heads a little bit forward because that position is more comfortable, and we can see all around us, which is especially important when we drive.

Whiplash injuries are, perhaps, the most common type of injury stemming from a motor vehicle collision, and because of that, they have acquired a bad connotation. Through the years, we have seen too many television shows featuring people pretending to have whiplash injuries or trying to milk their neck injuries. It has taken a toll on us, and juries now assume that those who use the word whiplash are lying about their injury or at least exaggerating it.

Of course, the insurance industry perpetuates this idea and spends millions of dollars in advertising and messaging to suggest, again, that whiplashes are not legitimate injuries and people injured in collisions try to cheat the system. Cases in which plaintiffs are caught faking an injury or putting together a fraudulent claim are publicized widely on TV and radio. That makes it more difficult for those who really do suffer from those injuries and are seeking compensation for them. The media coverage of fraudulent injury claims only serves to fuel skepticism.

Whiplash is therefore not a term I use very much and one I counsel my clients to avoid using themselves, even if they do have a neck injury caused by a rear-end collision. Whiplash is a perfectly correct medical term, and your doctor may use it. But I prefer to simply talk about what exactly happened to your neck. We can talk about whether or not muscles were torn when your head whipped back and popped forward again. We can talk about whether or not ligaments were torn. Was there any damage to your spine? Let's talk about those specific things rather than just relying on that suspicious and overused word whiplash. It carries too many negative connotations, and you do not want to be associated with people who would fake an injury.

DON'T REFER TO YOUR "PAIN AND SUFFERING"

Whiplash is not the only term that has acquired a negative connotation through the years. Another one is pain and suffering. Juries react very negatively to this one too, because the words have lost their original meaning and now are associated with the act of trying to milk injuries or embellish the consequences of the injuries. Juries have a predisposition to doubt all those who say they have experienced "whiplash," or are experiencing "pain and suffering." Of course many people experience all of these things when they are involved in a motor vehicle collision: whiplash and pain and suffering. But it is not wise to use those exact words. Talk specifically about your pain, and describe the things that you can no longer do or the hardships you endure because of your injury. Be specific. Do not just lump it all together in one lazy phrase of pain and suffering.

DO "EXPERIENCE" OR "FEEL" PAIN, BUT DON'T "COMPLAIN" OF PAIN

Commonly, doctors write in their medical records that a client "complained of" pain in his arm or neck or wherever. The patient "complained of" the pain. That is a fancy way of saying "mentioned." Again, it is a common medical term, but it carries negative connotations and therefore we try to keep it out of our case. At least, we try to not say it ourselves. The reality is that you simply "had" the pain, or you "experienced" it, or you "felt" it. Just because a doctor writes that you "complained of" a certain pain does not mean that you literally complained. You just told the doctor where it hurt when he asked you. Doctors could just as easily write, "Patient told me about a pain in his neck" or "Patient reported pain in his arm." The phrase "complained of" makes it sound as if the injured party is not cooperating with medical treatment and is a whiner. No one likes a whiner. That is why we never use the word complain or the phrase complained of when we refer to injuries. Your neck hurts or your back hurts. You are not complaining; you are simply stating a fact.

The insurance adjuster will most certainly use the word complain. He will ask a doctor flat-out if you "complained of" a certain injury and so will his attorney. And then he will turn around and tell the jury that you "complained of" something, just to make you sound like a "complainer," just to make you appear to not be badly hurt but just trying to milk your injuries. It is a very subtle thing to consider, but all of these words and phrases add up to a larger message. We always want that message to be clear and positive.

CONCLUSION

We have covered a great deal of material in this book, and much of it has been very specific, fine-tuned information that I have been honing for the better part of two decades, as an attorney. Some of these things may not stick with you, and that is why you should always keep this book close to you in case you ever need it again.

Hopefully, the bigger ideas will stick with you forever. The biggest one of all is that tractor-trailer collisions are different from all other motor vehicle collisions, including car versus car and even car versus smaller trucks. To put it succinctly, if a tractor-trailer is involved in a collision of any kind, that collision, that legal case, is in a class of its own.

It is not just the obvious things that make a tractor-trailer collision different. It is not just because tractor-trailers are much larger and much heavier than all other vehicles on the road. There are a number of other factors that make these cases different, and you need to be aware of these things in your own case so that you can get the best settlement award possible. When you know all of the fine points that make tractor-trailer cases different, you will know best how to investigate your case, how to work with your attorney (or on your own), and finally, how and when to settle. You will know if you are receiving the fair value of your case. A tractor-trailer collision is ten times more likely to be fatal than all other motor vehicle collisions, so naturally, in nonfatal tractor-trailer collisions, the injuries are also likely to be more severe.

Among the other things that are different about collisions involving tractor-trailers is the level of training the tractor-trailer driver should have had. The rules that apply to him are different from the rules that apply to normal automobile drivers like you and me. There are maintenance guidelines that apply to tractor-trailers too. Their drivers need to put forth extra effort to keep their vehicles safe and keep the general driving public out of harm's way. Traffic regulations mean something different to tractor-trailer drivers, simply because they affect tractor-trailers differently than they affect smaller vehicles. If a yellow speed limit sign suggests a speed of 35 miles per hour around a curve on a two-lane road, that suggestion is for the motorists driving sedans and coupes and pickup trucks; it is not meant for 18-wheelers. Tractor-trailer drivers should navigate that curve even more slowly and be extra cautious about the arc and path of the turn. Tractor-trailer drivers are held to a higher standard for a host of reasons, and all of the important ones are mentioned in this book.

More often than not I represent people who have been hit by a tractor-trailer, and that is usually an uphill climb. It is sometimes like David versus Goliath. We are David, and the trucking company is Goliath. This is one more way in which tractor-trailer cases are different. The resources they have are far greater than ours. This does not mean we are outmatched or have no chance of winning our case. It just means we have to work a little harder than they do and be a little smarter.

You may have read this book days or weeks after being in a wreck. Figuring out what you need to be doing can be overwhelming, and this is where an attorney can help. This book can help you do some things on your own—and most good attorneys will encourage you to do so—but in the end, you probably will be better off with the aid of an attorney. The trucking company and insurance company that you are up against would not dream of working on your case without legal counsel, and you should consider dealing with them through an attorney of your own. That is not to say that you have to; it is only to say that you should consider it. You get one shot at making yourself whole again after a wreck. Why not give it your best shot, using all of your available resources?

No one appreciates what truck drivers do for this country as much as I do. I completely respect the interstate system, the trucking industry, and the exchange of goods that those two great institutions allow every single day of the year. The good drivers—the safe ones—are the key to keeping our economy going, and if you ever were to get behind the wheel of a tractor-trailer, you would appreciate how complicated and difficult their job is. Forget about the sheer size of the vehicle, the blind spots, and the challenges of slowing down such a heavy moving object. Think just for one second about how difficult it would be to work your way through 18 gears. You think driving a five-speed stick shift is hard? Try 18. Or even 12. Try backing one of those trucks up.

The point is I am not here to vilify all truck drivers. Many of them do a good job and increase public safety and boost our economy in the process. (My father-in-law drove a truck for many years.) My argument is not about damaging the trucking industry—not at all. It is about making sure the trucking industry does its job safely—keeps us all safe—and is held accountable when its drivers are at fault and cause injury to others. We need to celebrate the good truck drivers and thank them. But it is just as important that we hold the bad ones accountable.

Many great truck drivers are under a tremendous amount of pressure from their companies to drive longer hours than they are supposed to. In those cases, we need to hold the trucking companies accountable as well. I have represented a number of truck drivers who were injured by the negligence of others, and so it is important that we all understand the rules of safety and adhere to them.

I enjoy what I do, and I have always been interested in being an attorney. I really enjoy representing people and being able to help them in their time of need. I love guiding them to a place where they can put their lives together after they have been involved in a collision. As for my specific area of law, well, that was probably influenced in part by events in my personal life. Both my sister and my wife were involved in serious traffic collisions before I became an attorney, and I have witnessed firsthand not only how traffic collision injuries can be life changing but also how trucking and insurance companies look for ways to avoid liability. They often try to mislead or even flat out invent things so they can settle cases for less than they are actually worth.

We are all part of building what has become one of the greatest countries the world has ever known. Our civil justice system is second to none, and I am proud to be a part of it. I have been representing people who have been injured in collisions for almost 20 years now. I worked for a number of years for a large personal injury firm, and when I set up my own firm, the smaller caseload allowed me to give more of my time to each case. I was also able to allocate more staff to each case and investigate things much more thoroughly. I was able to keep in better contact with my clients, be fully aware of their symptoms, and keep up with them throughout their medical treatment process. Working for myself and managing my own firm has made me a much better attorney.

There is no substitute for experience when it comes to jury trials, and I have found throughout my career how valuable that is. I understand more now than I understood 10 or 15 years ago, and although I was a pretty good trial attorney then, I am much better now. I know a lot more now about what really influences jurors and what judges are looking for. I also know how best to avoid going to trial in the first place. I know that being fully prepared to go to trial is the best way to avoid going to trial. I guess you could say that a good offense is the best defense.

The value of your case is never a fixed amount, as it would be in a worker's compensation case. There are dozens of variables, and the short answer is your case is worth as much as you can get for it. Your case is worth as much as a jury would give you for it. Often, these cases do not go before a jury, but the best plan is to hire an attorney and prepare your case as if it were heading to a trial before a jury. That way, you will have the strongest case possible, which will result in the best settlement for you. We first want to fix whatever needs attention in your body, and then we want to figure out what the rest of your case is worth, depending on how your injuries have affected your life.

There are a lot of things you can do on your own in your tractor-trailer collision case. You have many opportunities to help yourself and, ultimately, increase the value of your case. By following the advice put forth in this book, you can increase the value of your claim and get a lot of things started. It is a long process that leads to your collecting your rightful award and being made whole after your collision. But at a certain point, you will probably want to hire an attorney to help you with some of the procedures and strategies that you will face.

I hope the tips and strategies I have provided in this book are helpful. I hope you use them to your full advantage, whether you hire me as your attorney or not. Please feel free to e-mail me if you have any questions. Even if you are not interested in hiring me or any other attorney, I would be happy to answer any questions that you have. If you need an attorney in a different state, I do know many good trucking collision attorneys across the US and will be happy to give you their contact information and even introduce you if you prefer. I promise not to give you the hard sell. This is my life's work, and I believe in it. I respect the law, and I respect the trucking industry. My goal is always to hold people and companies accountable for the injuries they have caused my clients through negligence. Like my father, I am a defender of the underdog.

LAW OFFICES OF
ALAN LEVAR
INJURY LAWYERS

Three offices:

900 S. Shackleford, Suite 300
Little Rock, AR 72211
501-588-0082

208 N. 26th Street, Suite B
Arkadelphia, AR 71923
870-246-7070

505 Dave Ward Dr., Suite 2
Conway, AR 72032
501-358-5050

9 781599 325569